Stepdog

Stepdog

A MEMOIR

---•---

MIREYA NAVARRO

G. P. PUTNAM'S SONS
NEW YORK

PUTNAM

G. P. Putnam's Sons
Publishers since 1838
A Penguin Random House imprint
375 Hudson Street
New York, New York 10014

Library of Congress Cataloging-in-Publication Data

Navarro, Mireya.
Stepdog / Mireya Navarro.
p.   cm.
ISBN 978-0-399-16779-9
1. Dogs—Behavior.   2. Dogs—Psychology.   3. Jealousy.   4. Love.
5. Human-animal relationships—United States.   6. Navarro, Mireya—Marriage.
7. Stepparents—United States—Biography.   8. Dog owners—United States—Biography.
I. Title.   II. Title: Stepdog.
SF426.2.N38   2015   2014047108
636.7'0887—dc23

Printed in the United States of America
1   3   5   7   9   10   8   6   4   2

BOOK DESIGN BY AMANDA DEWEY

Penguin is committed to publishing works of quality and integrity.
In that spirit, we are proud to offer this book to our readers;
however, the story, the experiences, and the words
are the author's alone.

Some names have been changed to protect the privacy of the individuals involved.

For my mother, Dinorah, and my cousin Alma,
and for all the women who left me too soon
and those still in my life who continue to inspire me.

For stepmoms everywhere.

Contents

One

The Dog

underestimated the dog. On the first night I slept at my future husband's place in Los Angeles, Eddie peed outside the bedroom door.

"He's never done that," Jim said, mystified.

Jim rushed to get a cloth and cleaner to rub the yellow from the cream-colored carpet as I paid no attention whatsoever to the incident. I lingered in bed instead, savoring the memories of the night before and our moments together. I was visiting from New York and had just met the dog. What is there to say about a dog? A bit peculiar, no doubt, but he seemed harmless enough. In my bicoastal romance, the dog was an afterthought. What a dope I was. Love blinded me to the conniving manipulator behind the wagging tail.

Eddie was cute, I'll grant that much. About forty pounds, with dark spots on white fur, floppy ears, and a rump that looked absurdly comical in motion, Eddie never failed to draw oohs and aahs as he sniffed his way down the street. The spots appeared to be his charm and a great object of curiosity.

"What a cutie! What kind of dog is that?" people often asked.

"Just a junkyard dog," Jim replied proudly. He loved that his dog was manly, with a ferocious bark and, as I would soon discover, a taste for brawls. Jim could go on and on about his precious Eddie.

"Based on what our vet told us, he has the markings of an Australian cattle dog known as a blue heeler. The blue comes from that little bit of gray behind his ears. For some reason the gray is referred to as blue."

Fascinating.

". . . When he plays with other dogs, he nips at their haunches, which is a kind of herding mentality. Blue heelers have that instinct to herd cattle."

Jim liked to point out that he and Ralph Lauren had the same taste in dogs. But the blue heeler in a Ralph Lauren newspaper ad he showed me was a more regal blue heeler, and not just because he was posing next to an exquisite denim-and-tan-leather handbag. The elongated profile didn't look anything like Eddie's boxy head. Eddie seemed more pit bull–ish than blue heel–ish.

"That's Eddie's ancestor," Jim insisted. "That's his forebear."

Whatever. A disagreeable mutt—that's all Eddie really was. It took no time for him to drop the niceties. He behaved like a dog with Jim and a jealous mistress with me. All we had in common was that we loved the same man. When I fell in love with Jim, I had braced myself for stepkids. Never, ever, did I worry about a stepdog.

In case you're wondering, I'm not a cat person. I like dogs. In fact, I love dogs. Mitsuki, Tweety, Peluche, Rubi, Sophie, Jade, Esperanza, Bailey, Pinky, Canelo, Spencer, Riley, Bridget, Rani—these were dogs from my childhood and dogs that belonged to friends. They were loving and funny and made you happy. But these dogs usually knew they were dogs. They were the kind that are ecstatic to see you and jump around in circles and greet you like it's midnight on New Year's Eve. They don't ignore you or stress you out or play head games or kick you when you're down.

Initially, I ignored Eddie's passive-aggressiveness, although marking his territory outside Jim's bedroom was certainly creepy. But he soon became confrontational. He barked at the sight of me. He physically came between Jim and me when we tried to kiss or dance. He raced me or intercepted me when I approached Jim. When we shoved our way to our man, I usually won. Oh, could the mutt whimper. But Eddie had already beaten me to Jim by nearly four months. They met in January. I didn't show up until April. I was the intruder.

"What is your problem? What's wrong with you? Quiet! Stop it! Sit!"

It became apparent that a good chunk of my life would be squandered proving who was more alpha. Never show your fears! The rest of my time would be spent shooing Eddie away, tugging Eddie's leash, nagging Jim about Eddie, avoiding Eddie, and wanting to lose Eddie. It was exhausting.

I used to laugh watching one of my favorite sitcoms, *Frasier*. Dr. Frasier Crane hated his father's Jack Russell terrier, another piece of work also called Eddie.

"Must this dog stare at me all the time?" Frasier grumbled in one episode as the dog watched him playing the piano. Sometimes the two would get into stare-down contests. Hilarious.

I don't laugh anymore.

How can one person's source of comfort and affection be so objectionable to another? Some of us see the dog as a lovable companion but definitely a few ranks below humans. Others treat them as a favorite child or principal friend. Jim fit in between these perspectives, but we still had to reconcile our differences.

To me, Eddie was just a pet. To Jim, Eddie was family.

Dogs had never been on my checklist for sizing up boyfriend prospects. I was more worried about "cons" like "self-absorbed" or "cheap." Jim dazzled me with "pros." He was smart and loving and fun and sexy and caring. He was responsible and financially solvent. He didn't have male habits that grossed me out. Who cares about a dog? Anyone can get along with a little doggie. And if the dog was to become a problem, we could always find a more suitable arrangement. Humans always come first. Right? It wasn't like Eddie was any kind of deal-breaker. Jim didn't even mention him when we first met. Jim was not that kind of dog person. He wasn't like those people who make their dogs vet their dates. My Jim was normal.

Not his dog, though. What a sour personality Eddie had. He was aloof and generally unaffectionate to anyone but Jim. He refused to fetch. He licked mostly himself. He was sometimes more cat than dog. Not too bright, he was often more hamster than cat. A possessive hamster-cat. He made you long for a llama.

I'm not saying Eddie was a bad dog, necessarily. He didn't chew shoes. He didn't steal socks. He didn't destroy furniture or dig holes in the lawn or wake us up at dawn. He just hated me. Jim advised to woo him. I tried. But even after I walked Eddie and cleaned up after him and fed him and scratched his empty head, he would not extend his loyalty. There was just no scoring points with Eddie. He just wouldn't share Jim.

"Just ignore him," our soulmate said when I complained.

"How can I ignore him? He barks and growls at me, he tries to make me trip, his breath stinks . . ." Sometimes I would also catch him looking at me funny, like he was casting some canine spell. What a weirdo. ". . . he snores, he farts, he sheds, he walks into . . ."

At the sound of "walk," Eddie would perk up from his slumber and look at Jim.

"Is that true?" Jim would coo, scratching away. "Do you snore? Do you fart?"

Then, to me: "He's my pal."

Then, to Eddie: "Aren't you my buddy, you big galoot?"

I sometimes threatened to get my own pal, a cuddly pup that would be everything Eddie wasn't.

"Right," Jim said. "Eddie, meet lunch."

Obviously my prince was not about to gallop to meet me halfway.

To be fair, Eddie was not without charm. He didn't slobber. He didn't hump legs. His tongue didn't hang out except when it was really hot in the summer. And without Jim around he was, indeed, capable of being just a dog, more or less. Anytime Jim traveled for work, he left him in my care, and Eddie took no time in figuring out which side his bread was buttered on. He'd sprout angel wings and turn into new, improved Eddie. When it was just the two of us, he'd follow me as I went through my rounds between the den and the kitchen. He'd stand watch while I sat watching TV or he'd lie at my feet, making goo-goo eyes at me. If I absentmindedly crossed my legs as I worked at the computer, he'd ever-so-gently rest his head on my dangling foot, as if to say: "I can't be close enough to you."

It felt good being treated with love and respect. Then Jim would come back home and Eddie would dump me and resume hostilities.

Remember Marley's look of concern in the movie *Marley & Me*, when Jennifer Aniston came home after a miscarriage and sat quietly crying on her living room couch? Remember the dog sitting by her side, still as a rock, watching her every move, being there for her when she finally breaks down in convulsing sobs and buries her face in his fur? Eddie would have never done that. Eddie had only five settings: Walk. Sniff. Eat. Sleep. Inappropriately and noisily lick privates.

Yet we seldom hear about unlikable dogs like Eddie. We only hear, incessantly, about these holy best friends—these overachievers, even!—and the essential role they play in the household.

We have all read the stories about dogs becoming a healing presence for the sick and old. And they can be excellent companions. Jill Abramson, the former executive editor of *The New York Times*, wrote a series of stories for the newspaper's website, then a book, chronicling the first year of Scout, the golden retriever that replaced her other beloved dog, Buddy.

"My two children, who grew up with him but flew the nest years before his demise, joked that Buddy was my one perfect relationship in my life," she wrote.

This is what Clara, a friend from grade school who is now a radio personality, said of her "four-legged son" Alejandro Alberto (red flag: a dog with a middle name) in a newspaper profile:

"He died after sixteen years with me. I think that when we human beings learn that dogs are superior beings that are here on earth to teach us unconditional love, we'll hang our heads in shame."

"A cat teaches you dignity," she told her interviewer, "and a dog teaches you love that knows no limits."

Please.

It's not that I question these emotions. But a dog is a dog is a dog. We all know Alejandro Alberto's "superiority" and "unconditional love" would have been seriously tested at the sight of a steak. Not even. Cheetos. He'd ditch both owner and "unlimited" love for Cheetos.

Of course, it was unrealistic to expect much sympathy. Friends, coworkers, relatives—they were all in Eddie's corner.

"Poor Eddie. Can you guys get into counseling?" my friend Bill suggested when I shared my latest grievance. There is such a thing as pet-related therapy, of course, and Bill wasn't kidding. Never mind that his own life was run by two hyperactive "fur babies"—Jessica and Stanley, both Chihuahua mixes—that at one point got him and his partner, Scout, evicted from their apartment in Los Angeles because of a no-pets policy. As they frantically looked for a place to crash with their dogs right before the Christmas holiday, I suggested—helpfully, I thought—that they put the rescue dogs in a kennel to make the search for temporary housing easier.

Out of the question, Bill said. "They are our children."

And I'm the one who needs therapy. (Many years later, after marriage and two actual children, this is what Bill said to me one day: "Do you want Stanley? He's an idiot.")

Only my sister in Puerto Rico, Mari, a down-to-earth dog lover, would empathize and ask every now and then during our long-distance conversations: "Have you poisoned the dog yet?"

. . .

Clearly, I would never kill another living thing, not even Eddie. But in my new life as wife and stepmom, Eddie was no joke. He was another willful personality in the household, another tension in the "blended" family, the last straw on a bad day, the extra, unacceptable hardship that sometimes made me want to run away. He wasn't just a dog. He was negative energy, a competitor for my husband's attention, a nuisance, a bad roommate, a total traitor. Against my better judgment, he got under my skin.

At some point, it all got to be too much. I was utterly unprepared to gain an instant family, juggle so many new roles and relationships at once, and struggle with culture clashes. I had been so naive. For some reason I never doubted I would always get my way in my own marriage, just like I did when it was just me. I stepped into my new role ready to change things for the better, to teach the kids and love the husband and make everyone happy, fulfilled, and grateful I had come into their lives. That didn't turn out exactly as I'd envisioned.

And then there was this darn dog. There were so many times I could have used Eddie's allegiance, especially when I felt ganged up on or like an incompetent wife and stepmother. A sane dog would have offered comfort. But Eddie offered me none. No joy, no solace, no support, no love. He took sides right away and it wasn't with Team Mia. It would be me against four. I'd require a blended-family coach, and a shrink or two, to root for me.

One day I was in New York, longing for love but happily unmarried. The next I was in the suburbs of Los Angeles juggling a new job assignment, a husband, two stepkids in their tweens, and doggie dearest.

I, in good faith, endeavored to work things out. How hard could it be when I had already succeeded in finding true love?

So I tried and tried—with the husband, and the kids, and especially Eddie, who at least didn't talk back. I tried to tolerate Eddie. I tried to be friends with Eddie. I tried to train Eddie. And when that didn't work, I tried to (legally) get rid of Eddie. If someone had to go, it sure as hell wasn't going to be me.

But I'm getting ahead of myself. Just know I count on you to see my side.

Two

Mia Meets Jim

Jim and I first crossed paths one infernal summer in Phoenix. Until then, this tropical island girl never knew 100-degree heat that slapped you in the face. Mid-eighties was more my speed. I returned to my hotel room after a hectic day of workshops, panels, and job fair duty and the telephone message light was blinking.

"Hi, it's Jim Sterngold, a colleague of yours from the *Times*. I'm in Phoenix working on a story and I just ran into some of the *Times* people. If you're free for a drink, I'd love to meet you."

How collegial of Mr. Sterngold. He was making time to meet me in the middle of his breaking news story.

I was there for the National Association of Hispanic Journalists convention. While I took refuge at the air-conditioned Hyatt Regency, Jim was covering the story of a crazy arsonist who had been burning down new houses on the fringes of the city.

We had both worked for *The New York Times* as reporters for years but managed to never meet. When I got to the paper in 1989 from the San Francisco *Examiner*, he was already immersed in language training for his new assignment in Tokyo as a *Times* foreign correspondent. He left for Asia as I arrived in New York. He was now based in Los Angeles.

Then, in Arizona, of all places—actually, in a hotel bar in Arizona, of all places—I met my future husband. We had agreed to meet in the lobby bar, where the journalists gathered to drink and catch up. The bar was bustling with dark-haired people in business attire with name cards hanging from their necks. I took a high chair at one of the round tables with some acquaintances from the *Daily News*, *El Diario*, *La Prensa*, and others in the New York contingent, and waited. I didn't know what to expect. Nice colleague? Self-absorbed bore? Competitive foe? Certainly not a hottie, but when I saw him I was instantly attracted. Not too tall, but slim and athletic. Blue eyes, full lips. Sandy-colored hair, gray at the temples. Hirsute, a weakness. Very sexy.

Unlike some of the nerds back in the office—Seersucker Day, anyone? (not to be confused with Tie Tuesday!)—this James was almost Bondian. He was the kind of man I'd immediately notice at a party. He looked me straight in the eye with a couple once-overs. I couldn't help going into self-conscious dating mode as I shook his hand and made introductions. I held my vodka with a teeny splash of cranberry that barely tinted the clear liquid and worried he'd think

I was a heavy-drinking barfly. No one offered him their seat—way to go, New Yorkers!—but Jim was completely at ease. He politely offered to buy us drinks and went to the bar for his beer.

"So what's the story in Phoenix?" I said when he returned, trying to sound casual.

"Strange story," he said. "They had a bunch of arsons . . ."

What a deep, guttural radio voice. How old can he be with that sexy salt-and-pepper chest hair? I looked into his eyes and nodded.

". . . The guy left messages behind claiming that his fires were symbolic acts to protest the degradation of the desert by avaricious developers and he became a local folk hero. Except that after he was arrested, he turned out to be just a nut without a cause. Oops!"

He laughed. His teeth were perfect.

My gorgeous colleague was not only smart, he was self-deprecating and funny. I wasn't about to waste any more time talking shop. I quickly learned that he was divorced, had two kids, and loved opera and Santa Fe. That last bit came up because I told him I had enrolled in a summer course on opera at St. John's College in Santa Fe and would be seeing *Lucia di Lammermoor.* I had never been to Santa Fe.

"You'll enjoy it," Jim said of the city's famous opera house. "I've been there. It's a beautiful outdoor venue, with a tentlike roof, in a gorgeous area, and has fantastic food. I'm jealous. I wish I could join you."

Hands down, best prospect I had ever met in a bar. Just as I was letting my guard down, Jim excused himself, saying he had an early flight back to L.A. Oh, no! So soon? Then I remembered.

"I may see you soon," I said. "The national desk is sending me to L.A. for a month to fill in for Todd after he moves to D.C."

Todd, the chief of the L.A. bureau, was relocating to Washington.

As fate would have it, I had gotten his gig while they searched for his replacement.

Jim looked happily surprised. "Really? If you love the outdoors, you'll love L.A. There's great hiking and camping, and the weather is always fantastic."

Camping? I'd rather have every pore of my body waxed and then tattooed.

"I love camping!" I said.

This was just too much good fortune. My arsonist-hunter was already hinting at dates in the wilderness.

Later that night, as I dozed off playing back the reel of our encounter, I was mindful that if I dated Jim I would be violating one of my rules. I adhered to a never-date-coworkers policy and it had served me well. Who needs to see their walking mistakes at the office? But Jim and I worked on different coasts, so who needs a policy? And I wasn't after a relationship, particularly, just some spice in my otherwise uneventful love life at the moment.

My previous relationships had been phenomenally ill-suited to my ambition for everlasting love. I dated a charming alcoholic for more than two years. I dated a line cook who was too young, too bald, too overweight, but, oh, could he salsa dance. I stupidly agreed to go out with my mortgage broker—and stopped seeing him upon realizing he was a handsome misanthrope—before securing the loan. (At least he was ethical and I still got the loan.) Then I wasted another year of my youth on an intriguing Eastern European I met at a club. This guy was really hard to resist. He regaled me with stories about his hometown and urged me to read *The Master and Margarita* by Mikhail Bulgakov, his favorite book. He took me to shows and dinners at social clubs in unfamiliar corners of New York with flavored vodkas and spectacularly beautiful women. He lavished money and romance on me. Then one day I discovered that he packed a gun for protection. I wondered, "Protection from whom?"

The suspicions were reinforced one evening when he met me sporting a busted lip.

"What happened?"

He knew these people up in the Bronx, you see. He was so underpaid at his job, you know. He needed to make extra money, and these people, well, they knew how to get maximum insurance benefits. So, anyhoo, why not pack the car with relatives and purposely crash it into a tree?

"Taxi!"

My dating record was not stellar. I knew women who planned to get married by thirty and have kids by thirty-five. They were as strategic about love as they were about their careers. That wasn't me. I wasn't that well organized. I was just open to new adventures, to whatever life would bring in between newspaper deadlines.

And it wasn't like I was the Bachelorette. The pickings were always slim, even in college. At five-nine, I was too tall for a third of the men. Another third fell off because I had the better job. Finding the last third entailed online dating, which I tried without posting a picture, which any online dater knows will yield worse results than a two-dollar scratch-off lotto ticket. But I was too self-conscious for a picture. My pitch didn't help either. Determined to tell the truth, I wrote something along the lines of "Tall, slim Latina with zest for life and brains to match. Funny. Outspoken. Spanish accent. Loves jazz, good wine, assertive men."

I scared the deer.

I was aware I might have come across as a handful to some men, but I listened to Oprah. She once told Serena Williams on her show that women erred when they tried to dim their light to let their men shine. Blind the hell out of them, Oprah said, or something to that effect. The right man would be able to take all your brightness. Amen.

When I was young and still in Puerto Rico, before leaving for college in the States in my sophomore year, I wondered if I would be happy marrying and having kids in my twenties, like a good Puerto Rican girl. I grew up the oldest of two sisters in a suburb of San Juan, went to the same Catholic parish school from kindergarten to my senior year of high school, and should have had a couple toddlers by my big 3-0. That's what my sister, Mari, did, and today she and I are grateful for her three kids, my three adorable nephews, even if her marriage foundered.

Family is a big part of how we view ourselves. I religiously spent every New Year's Eve in Puerto Rico with my parents, sister, nephews, and assorted cousins and aunts and uncles. On the island and in the States, some of my closest friends were classmates from kindergarten and grade school—Diana, Celia, Lourdes, Clemson, Jesús—another extended family. Because of my upbringing in an extremely family-centric culture, I have never been afraid of commitment, just of bad husbands—specifically, hard-drinking, horse-betting, womanizing macho men that are not uncommon in Puerto Rican culture. Many men regarded their financial support of their family as a job well done. They did minimum housework or child-rearing and dropped everything come "Social Friday"—a Puerto Rican tradition that involves binge drinking until early Saturday. My father, a claims analyst with a health insurer, was among those partaking of our cultural traditions. His drinking drove a wedge between us as I grew up. I couldn't accept the loud personality that came with it, or the time and money wasted on it (and on gambling at the racetrack). I couldn't accept that it took my father—a good-natured, affectionate, and decent man when sober—away from me. And I couldn't accept it on behalf of my mother, who was more tolerant of it than I but was unhappy, still. I fought back with disrespect and the silent treatment.

My mother always worked, first as a secretary for a bread company and later as an administrative assistant in a doctor's office, and she called the shots in the house. But she didn't earn a lot and regretted not being financially independent enough to have options of her own. She worked full-time, she raised me and my sister, and she was the one who insisted we attend a Catholic parish school with Franciscan nuns from Pittsburgh, Pennsylvania, so we could learn English, even if she and my father had to scrape to pay for it. She hosted family gatherings, planned our beach vacations around the island, painted the house and made repairs, but she still needed my father's paycheck. I grew up with her mantra etched in my brain: "Get an education so you never have to depend on a man."

I looked up to my mom for her work ethic, common sense, and devotion to her family. I also learned from Mami to value my girlfriends. Even as an adult, I sometimes tagged along with her and the moms of my grade school buddies who met in restaurants or at one another's homes to drink rum and Cokes, gossip, and trash their husbands. They called themselves Las Muchachas—the girls—forever ageless. Their daughters, my contemporaries, all eventually got married in their twenties and had their own kids. We formed our own circle of friendship. Las Muchachitas. I always assumed I'd have children. I got crushes on babies. But I also wanted a partner to have children with, and that was the glitch. Adopting a baby by myself, like some of my friends have done, was not for me. I didn't feel that wanting or count myself that brave. And my job was a huge distraction from any long-term planning.

I had initially wanted to be a doctor. When revulsion at dissecting frogs in biology class made me reconsider, I spent months searching for a new major. Pharmacy? Accounting? Political Science? Then I saw *All the President's Men* as an impressionable nineteen-year-old premed student at the University of Puerto Rico and that was that. Until then, I had no idea there was such a profession as "Woodward and Bernstein." After watching the movie, all I wanted was to be a *Washington Post* reporter and knock on doors to dig for information, meet sources in parking lots, use code words and potted-plant signals to maintain secrecy, and publish stories that would dislodge the corrupt and make our world better. It didn't cross my mind I could suck at it. I was what you'd call an upbeat teenager, even if sometimes I wondered, "Is this all there is?" In those moments, I felt the smallness of the island and yearned for everything I didn't know. I also yearned for boys taller than me. I had been five-six by age twelve, five-nine by fifteen—taller than even my teachers. In other words, a skinny, flat-chested freak in a culture where men prefer to tower over their curvy women. I kept growing and slouching like Olive Oyl, and at some point my always enterprising mom got me what, to the naked eye, resembled a straightjacket to pull my shoulders back. She also enrolled me in modeling classes at Sears. "For your posture," she said. *"Siempre estas joroba."* Studying journalism in Washington, D.C., where I already had friends at Georgetown University, was my chance to step out of my flat shoes and sheltered life, if only for a few years of college.

I was oblivious to the fact that I could barely speak English. I couldn't even figure out the lyrics in disco songs. I could read and write it, though, thanks to the American nuns who enunciated at Colegio San Antonio, my parish school. I was going for Woodstein, not Barbara Walters, so I picked my new major and told my parents I had to move to the States for a little while because the UPR had no undergraduate journalism program. Amazingly, they said yes. These were the same parents who, on my first date with an eighteen-year-old, who picked me up honking from a yellow convertible Corvette, insisted on chaperoning me, which is how I came to be French-kissed at fifteen for the first time in a dark movie theater with Mom and baby sister sitting just a few rows away. But somehow, the idea of sending me off alone to the States still in my teens didn't scare them. As long as it involved education, my mom, and therefore my dad, was fine with it. Neither of them had gone to college, and they both wanted it for their daughters.

And there was my mom's "Get your education so you never have to depend on a man."

I guess it's no mystery why I stayed single for so long.

Above all, I was trusted. It was as if Mami and Papi could foretell that their oldest would go through college without smoking pot and with her virginity intact. As I prepared to leave the island, I knew I'd be homesick. But I was ready for the non-Caribbean world. I applied to George Washington University in Washington, D.C., and enrolled with a patchwork of financial aid—scholarships, loans, work-study programs—and whatever my parents could give me. Once in D.C., finances were the least of my problems. That first year at GW was T-O-U-G-H. I lived in a huge, noisy, awful dorm. Every weekend, drunk students would pull the fire alarm a few times a night, so we all spent a good part of the year freezing in our bathrobes out on the street while firefighters checked the building for smoke. I had several roommates, one of them a nymphomaniac. At least that was my humble opinion as the only virgin in the zoo. We'll call her Betsy. She slept around as if it were a required course. It's as if she had been held hostage for years by her parents and was finally tasting freedom. I didn't care until she brought a guy to our room and had sex right below me on the bunk bed.

"Sheet, Betsy!" I said the next morning in my heavy accent. "You can't do theeese!"

Betsy found me immensely funny, which made me angrier and less fluent. All I could do was move my half of the bunk bed to the study alcove in our room and the next year get out of campus housing altogether. I found a studio apartment with mice above a Roy Rogers chicken restaurant and roomed with a Puerto Rican high school classmate who was as celibate as I was.

That first year I could barely keep up with classes, and my journalism school grades were in the gutter. I had the hardest time with accents that didn't sound like mine. I went to cover Jimmy Carter during a presidential campaign appearance for an assignment and didn't understand a word he said. (I taped him and a friend later interpreted his drawl for me.)

But I was lucky to find a mentor in a beloved professor who everyone knew as Puff, short for Puffenbarger.

Charles Puffenbarger was a business editor at *The Washington Post* who also mentored one of my Watergate heroes, Carl Bernstein, and brought him to class as a speaker. I was so impressed I went out with Puff for a whole year after the course ended. Our relationship was flirtatious, not sexual, but Puff convinced me I could be a good journalist and our friendship endured for twenty years, until he died of brain cancer at seventy. Puff encouraged me to aim high. My grades steadily improved as my English got better. I interned at the Cox Newspapers bureau in Washington and got a few pieces published in *The Washington Post.*

Then, as I was set on returning home, I happened to spot an ad for a summer journalism program for minority journalists at the University of California at Berkeley. A summer in sunny California? I applied, got in, and bought new sunglasses. I had no idea the Bay Area has miserably cold weather in the summer. Neither did I realize until it was too late that the benignly named "summer program" was really a boot camp. Basically, top journalists around the country—the likes of Bob Maynard, Nancy Hicks, Eileen Shanahan, Les Payne, Roy Aarons, Milton Coleman, and many others—came to Berkeley on two-week rotations to kick our butts. They edited a weekly called *Deadline* and we spent the week reporting and writing for it in between seminars about the ethics and standards of our chosen profession. I had never worked so hard in college or life. I also realized I had overlooked an important detail. The program wanted to increase racial diversity in newsrooms, so they wanted me to interview for jobs on the mainland. I told my parents I had to delay my return for a couple years. I told them the experience in the States would help me land an even better job back home. My parents were all for it.

But I never returned home.

My poor parents. They never thought they'd lose me forever by sending me to college. Neither did I. I don't regret my choices, but it would forever gnaw at me that I chose to not have my family around for most of my adult life—or any of my old close friends, for that matter. Phone calls and twice-a-year visits could never make up for all the moments lost. I thought more about this only as I got older. When you live apart from the family you love, by choice, nostalgia only grows with time. But as a twenty-one-year-old suddenly in charge of her own life, I was just excited, even if I cried on the plane all the way to San Francisco from San Juan when I officially moved out of the parental home for good to start my first real job. That would be as a reporter for William Randolph Hearst's San Francisco *Examiner*, an afternoon paper in a city I came to love so much that it took me another ten years to think about moving again.

I fell in love with San Francisco at first sight. It was hilly and surrounded by water just like home. The fog and perennial chill were definite downsides. But the city more than made up for those with its sheer physical beauty, its accepting politics, and its racial integration. I arrived in a shell-shocked city, though. Just a few months earlier, San Francisco mayor George Moscone and supervisor Harvey Milk had died at the hands of Dan White. And just days before those shootings, Peoples Temple cult leader Jim Jones orchestrated the mass murders and suicides in Guyana.

On my first day at the *Examiner*, they assigned me a desk near Tim Reiterman, a reporter who was shot in that tragedy but survived the same hail of bullets that killed Congressman Leo Ryan on a remote jungle airstrip. He was friendly and kind to the new wide-eyed hire, just like the rest of the *Ex*'s staff.

My colleagues were eccentrics, cynics, union rabble-rousers, musicians, chili cook-off experts, and brilliant writers, some even more so after a liquid lunch at the corner hangout bar, the M&M. The paper itself promoted fun. It gave the staff free tickets to Giants games at frigid Candlestick Park. It sponsored opera at Golden Gate Park. It threw lavish Christmas parties with exhilarating quantities of Dungeness crab. The newsroom was so loosey-goosey that I would blithely indulge in pot smoking—finally!—with another editor at the end of our midnight shift in the city editor's office, right next to a bustling copy desk. If they smelled something, they said nothing. One night, in the high of very strong weed, I drove over the Bay Bridge to go home to the cozy basement with a fireplace I rented in the house of my friends Laura and Larry in Oakland. The ride was always smooth late at night, but this time I became so paranoid that I thought the car in the rearview mirror was following me—like *really* following me. I rolled down the window hoping that a blast of chilly air would sober me up, then remembered from some news story that the California Highway Patrol spots drunks by their rolled-down windows. I rolled the window back up and turned up the radio and sang gibberish to whatever was playing at the top of my lungs to make it over the five-mile bridge and up the Oakland hills. I cleared the bridge only to run into the cop car that was always stationed at the intersection of the commercial village of Montclair, which I had to pass to get home. They were there to keep an eye on the comings and goings of Huey P. Newton of the Black Panthers, who lived in the vicinity. That night I became bridge-phobic. I soon quit pot and moved to San Francisco, to a nice one-bedroom near Golden Gate Park, only fifteen minutes away from the office over solid ground.

I was growing up on the job too. Over ten years at the *Ex*, I pretty much covered every beat and every story. My Spanish was highly valued, especially since the city became a cradle of the sanctuary movement for undocumented immigrants escaping the American-financed wars in Central America. I got sent to Mexico City for the 1985 earthquake that killed ten thousand people, arriving early enough to experience terrifying aftershocks that leveled buildings. And I was almost killed in a road ambush when the *Ex* sent me to Nicaragua for a series of stories as the Sandinista government fought the American-financed contras.

That close call cured me from ever aspiring to be a foreign correspondent again. Some reporters feel a personal responsibility to tell war stories. They relate on a human level to the misery of others no matter where they are in the world. I realized I cared more about reporting about the problems at home. I wanted to expose and, I hoped, affect our own injustices—discrimination, racism, income inequality. Those were the stories that fed my commitment to journalism. The next time I would do any more war coverage, the war would find me—on a crisp September morning at home in New York City.

But by the late 1980s, I was at a career crossroads. I had taught college journalism classes but wasn't interested in teaching full-time just yet. I had so much to learn myself. I still loved journalism but was young enough to pursue a whole new career if I wanted to. I didn't know what to do, so I went back to school, this time on a year-long journalism fellowship at the University of Michigan in Ann Arbor. It led me to renew my vows to journalism and pursue *The New York Times*, which I joined exactly ten years after I first walked into the newsroom at the *Examiner*.

I was sad to abandon my adopted tribe at the *Ex* and a tad scared about moving to New York. The only time I had lived there was a summer during college under a student program. I worked for the telephone company in New Jersey and lived in an NYU dorm on Fifth Avenue. I had loved the bustle of Washington Square Park, walking everywhere, shopping for earrings among street vendors, discovering the bizarre appeal of *The Rocky Horror Picture Show* and *Oh! Calcutta!* But now I'd be returning as an adult with a sense of mission. New politics, new players, new weather (how do reporters cover news in the snow?), new bosses. You never know with new bosses.

Fortunately, my *Times* editors in Metro—the metropolitan news section that covered the city (along with its region and the state government upstate in Albany) and competed with the "Headless Body in Topless Bar" headlines of the tabloids—were pretty great, as I had to prove myself all over again. They were supportive, smart, and, for the most part, white men in suits. The *Times* was not exactly multicultural back then.

But in the late 1980s, New York was a stark departure from the way it was in the 1940s, when mostly rural Puerto Ricans first began to leave the island in waves for manufacturing jobs in the city that soon disappeared, creating an underclass that persists in some pockets today. The city was different from the days when my Titi (Aunt) Lucy and Tío (Uncle) Luis had to pass themselves off as Italians to get their apartment in Ozone Park in Queens. Or when my cousin Mayrah lived in the urban war zone known as Alphabet City in the East Village, before it gentrified with bistros and cupcake shops. New York was a nicer city than the one my relatives survived—with the added benefit that it came with my Titi Lucy, Tío Luis, and my cousin Mayrah!

I needed an apartment, but the search was painful. I couldn't tell prewar from postwar, and the massive brick buildings all looked equally ugly. But once inside the buildings, the trade-offs were more obvious. I held out for good light and a kitchen that could accommodate a normal-size refrigerator. In the buyer's market of the late 1980s, there were good choices at prices I could afford. After months of looking and indecision, I moved into a bright and spacious rental on the Upper West Side two blocks from Central Park. I was doomed to hearing sirens and honking day and night, but I could at least see sky from the windows and jog around the reservoir.

I missed the Bay Area terribly, but I eventually found mini–New Yorks that were manageable, wonderful, and friendly. I remember the exact moment I realized I had ceased missing San Francisco and became a New Yorker. I was in the back of a cab on my way home, a little tipsy from a night out with friends, when we stopped at a light, right in front of the most beautiful produce and flower display on a sidewalk market. The oranges and reds, greens and yellows just popped, and in my daze, perhaps because the fruits and veggies reminded me of California, I thought, "I love New York."

Then I moved.

I was happy in New York, had a boyfriend and close colleague friends and my Latina women's group (LIPS) and the theater and Central Park and a gig as adjunct professor at Columbia University's graduate school of journalism. But the *Times* offered me the job of Miami bureau chief, and my mentor at the paper, Gerald Boyd, urged me to take it, wanting me to be strategic about my career. I couldn't pass this assignment up, he told me. I was reluctant to move to Florida barely five years after settling in New York and adjusting to its craziness, but Miami had two big draws aside from the promotion: my sister, her husband, and their two boys lived there; and Puerto Rico would be part of my beat. Not only would I get to travel to the island frequently for stories, but I'd also live close to my family again, so close that I had the chance to hold my third nephew, Alexander, as a newborn, a joy I missed with the first two.

Florida was big and busy and meant constant travel. Who knew the state is big enough to have two time zones? Hurricanes. Fidel and the Cuban exiles. Cuba and Guantánamo. The ValuJet crash. Versace's murder. The declawed lion that escaped from a zoo in Orlando. At some point my hair started falling out in clumps and I got shingles.

When my Florida assignment drew to a close on the fifth year, I got to spend seven months covering Central America and the Caribbean for the foreign desk while they looked for a replacement for that beat. As I wrapped up, I was grateful for an amazing run. What a memorable five years of reporting. But when I was offered San Francisco next, a dream job had it come a decade earlier, all I wanted was to go back home—to New York. I didn't want to live so far from my family again—a full day of travel from San Francisco to San Juan. I wanted to travel for work, but just occasionally. After I moved back to New York, I soon was headed for Houston for a six-month detour to follow three businessmen—black, white, and Latino—for the "How Race Is Lived in America" series, a collaboration by a team of writers that won a Pulitzer. I then decamped to Washington Heights at the upper tip of Manhattan, to a cozy apartment by the Hudson River, for good.

Then I met Jim.

Three

9/11: Taking Stock

Jim and I said good-bye in Phoenix and I didn't hear from him again. I didn't really expect to, since we were just colleagues who had run into each other by chance. But L.A. now beckoned like never before. I had welcomed my temporary assignment in Los Angeles as a chance to report on new subjects in an area of the country I didn't really know. San Francisco and Los Angeles were so different in geography and zeitgeist that their two populations were notoriously oblivious to each other. In my many years in the Bay Area, I had been to L.A. twice at the most. If you lived in San Francisco, there was no reason to go to Los Angeles, and vice versa. Now I had two good reasons to brave the spread of what I used to know as la-la land. Jim awaited, or so I thought.

On my first day in the *Times*'s L.A. bureau, my dreamboat greeted me warmly. He offered me a tour of the office and introduced me to the eight other colleagues who worked there.

"Over here, the fax machine," Jim said as I followed like a giddy puppy. With the flair of a magician, he opened an upper cabinet in the kitchen. Ta-da! The shelves were stuffed with snacks. "Here's where we keep our stash of Oreos." He grinned. "In the morning, the office manager buys doughnuts from Bob's in the farmers' market. Do you like glazed or jelly?"

Talk about sweet!

All correspondents had the luxury of their own private offices, but Todd had not moved out yet, so I staked out a corner of the common area near the office manager's desk by the front door. I soon got started on a couple stories, befriended the manager, Catherine, and forgot about my surroundings. I cared more about the apartment I had found just blocks from the ocean and the shopping promenade in Santa Monica. The sight of water felt like home. I woke up every day to impossibly perfect weather. Every single day. Driving against traffic (to my surprise, the bulk of commuters headed away from downtown Los Angeles toward the Pacific Coast Highway), I had a short commute to the *Times* bureau in the mid–Wilshire Boulevard area. No one came in before nine a.m. except for Andy, the biotech reporter, who typically was the first one in and the last one out no matter how bright the sun shone outside. I knew this because I was in the perfect spot to see the comings and goings of my colleagues. Jim and I saw each other every day, trading hellos, smiles, and stolen glances. I bode my time, waiting for my handsome office guide to ask me out to lunch. Then I waited some more. Then—nothing. The invitations never came. Camping? I wished.

Jim spent the days out on the street reporting or holed up in his office, and soon there was not even casual conversation. Even when we sat next to each other at Todd's send-off over lunch at Morton's, roasting our colleague and joking about a celebrity two tables over we couldn't place (Judith Light)—nothing.

Much later Jim would explain that he was involved with someone at the time and didn't want to complicate things. But, he asked, hadn't I noticed that he had carved a path on the carpet from the many trips he took to the office pantry just so that he could walk by my desk and catch a glimpse of me? Frankly, I had not, distracted as I was by disappointment and desire.

I was crestfallen. My L.A. fantasy failed to materialize. I moved on. I spent some quality time with my friends Rose, a news editor with the *Press-Telegram* in Long Beach, and Gabriel, a Hollywood publicist who let me tag along for some fun red-carpet events. And I was busy at work. One story took me to the famous border fence between Mexico and the United States that ends in the ocean off the California shore. Driving there, I passed billboards showing the silhouettes of a man, a woman, and a little girl with pigtails clinging to her mother's hand as they ran. It was a disconcerting warning: watch out for illegal immigrants attempting to cross the freeway. That certainly put my little personal disappointments in perspective.

Still, I flew back to New York deflated. A month—a whole month!—could have been used so productively. We could have had romantic dinners at Inn of the Seventh Ray in Topanga Canyon. We could have strolled around the Getty Museum and hiked the Santa Monica Mountains. We could have driven along the coast to the

Santa Barbara wine country and stopped at the Hitching Post on the way back for a dinner of steak and grilled artichokes, downed with the restaurant's own pinot noir. We could have fallen in love and planned a future together. I tried to shrug it off. His loss.

I was still moping two weeks later when, on a clear, picture-perfect Tuesday morning in New York, the phone woke me up.

"Are you okay?" It was my sister, calling from Puerto Rico.

"Yes, why?"

"Turn on the TV and call me back."

I made it to the living room in time to watch the World Trade Center being swallowed up by dust. God help us. I sat frozen, weirdly fixated on how the towers fell. I don't know how long it took me to come to and realize that on clear days I could see the buildings from my roof. I lived by the Hudson River on the top floor of a thirteen-floor co-op in Washington Heights. I raced one flight up the stairs. A few neighbors were already gathered on the southern side of the roof, watching the spectacle in silence.

After I don't know how long, I suddenly remembered. "Shit. The *Times!*" The newsroom must have been going nuts, and here I was, one of their metropolitan news reporters, watching the tragedy unfold in my bathrobe. I rushed down the stairs and got a strangely calm Metro deputy editor on the line.

"Just find your way there," he said, Zenlike.

I dressed quickly and headed out on foot. With no car or bike to my name, and no yellow cabs or town cars in sight and all public transportation shut down, I would have to walk twelve miles south to get to what would soon become known as Ground Zero. I started walking but I never made it to the disaster site. Half a block from my apartment I saw small huddles of people on street corners talking, some of them crying. I opened my notebook and started taking notes. A few blocks south, a crowd of hundreds had gathered at the foot of the George Washington Bridge, many of them men and women in work clothes and holding briefcases.

These commuters from New Jersey were not going to wait around for the city to shake itself back to normal. They had walked uptown and now wanted to walk some more, over the Hudson, to go back home to safety and hug a loved one tight. It all felt dreamlike. There was the bar with overhead TV sets packed with people drinking hard liquor at ten in the morning. There was the Arab convenience store owner in tense conversation with a customer about who had done it. Lines of residents crowded grocery stores and ATMs as if they were preparing for a hurricane. And I heard the name Osama bin Laden more than a few times out of New Yorkers' lips from day one.

I had not advanced even a mile when I called the newsroom again. "I'm still uptown, but there's so much going on I think I should stay here."

"Start filing," an editor said.

Which I did, along with hundreds of my colleagues. Nothing went to waste. We put in the paper everything we heard and saw. Our vignettes ran under the headline: "A Day of Terror: The Voices; Personal Accounts of a Morning Rush That Became the Unthinkable." After that day, we stayed on overdrive for months and months, in my case covering funerals and reporting and writing short profiles of the missing and the dead. Known as Portraits of Grief, these mini-profiles were solely based on the remembrances of relatives, friends, and coworkers. These mini-eulogies were not traditional journalism.

We didn't do much digging. But 9/11 was not a traditional story. We were acknowledging each and every victim among the thousands of lives lost.

I wrote two or three profiles a day. These interviews put me in the midst of the horror as it unfolded. Some stories were more horrible than others. A young husband who worked in one of the towers along with his wife told me that when the first plane hit, his wife had panicked and wanted to leave the building. As they stood by the elevators trying to decide what to do, the voice from a loudspeaker said that everybody should return to their offices. She still wanted to go, but he convinced her to stay. The young husband cried his tale into the phone as I told him how sorry I was and took notes and wondered how this widower in his twenties could ever be happy again.

And since traditional journalism was out the window, I said yes when a widow from Stamford, Connecticut, asked me if we could please run the portrait of her husband, a broker-dealer named Randolph Scott, on the day of what would have been their wedding anniversary, which was coming up shortly. I remember going to Stamford one weekend to visit my friend Celia and how I froze at the scene at the train station: the parking lot was filled with unclaimed cars belonging to commuters who never returned home. I wrote the portrait of Randolph Scott and arranged for it to run on the specified day. Except, that Saturday, when I opened the paper, the name of the wife had been changed from Denise to Nancy. What the hell?!!!

I called the office in a panic, but no one could explain what had happened. All I could do was call Denise Scott and self-flagellate. She was extremely nice about it. In fact, she said, she had been hearing jokes about her husband's "other wife" all day long and the laughter helped her get through her painful anniversary. I sent her flowers on behalf of the *Times* and the paper republished the portrait with the correct name. I chalked up these strange mistakes to the fact that although journalists are supposed to behave like detached, objective automatons in the face of unspeakable acts, we sometimes crack. We were all deeply affected, not always in obvious ways, in the newsroom, just like everybody else. From the relative safety of our office many blocks away, near Times Square (I now worried the *Times* could be a likely target for another terrorist attack), I wrote portrait after portrait through the end of 2001.

As reporters, we often don't know how our stories land, what impact they may have on individual readers. One late night, as I absentmindedly flipped TV channels, I stumbled upon a local talk show where a father was talking about his son, another 9/11 casualty. The name sounded familiar, and then I realized I had written about the son. The father mentioned the portrait and the interviewer asked how he had liked it.

"It was beautiful," he said, bursting into tears.

I burst into tears too.

That day left New Yorkers nervous wrecks, always jumpy and on the alert, suspicious of the solitary paper bag left on a subway train, of a backpack with no owner beside it. And others who suffered personal losses lived through a never-ending tragedy. A friend waited for her mother's remains and possessions to be found bit by bit. Another friend, my colleague Dana, lost her love and the father of her only child in the wars that followed, left to raise her baby son alone. That baby would grow up beautiful and healthy and experiencing his father's absence to the core. The rest of us could only learn to appreciate our loved ones even more. I also took stock of what a bitch I had been to some people. I thought about a boyfriend I had loved very much in my twenties and almost married, but had discarded in a manner I now regretted. I looked him up on Facebook and found him, happily married with kids. I called him not to apologize but to tell him that I remembered him, that I was grateful for having had him in my life, and that his happiness made me happy. I don't know if the words came out right, but from then on I was conscientious about nurturing relationships and never taking those who mattered to me for granted. At least I'd try.

Mired in the aftermath of terrorism, I hardly paid attention when I heard through the grapevine that the new executive editor of the *Times* had decided to clean house and replace a bunch of national reporters with his own picks.

Four

Sparks and Fireworks
(And No Crazy Dog)

I ran into Jim one morning in the newsroom. He looked beaten.

"What are you doing here?" I asked cheerfully, genuinely glad to see him.

We had not been in touch since my stint in the L.A. bureau, and he had been out of my mind. But when I saw him I blushed.

He mumbled something and looked even more miserable. He told me he had just been told he could not stay in Los Angeles and had to transfer back to New York.

"Do you want to have a drink after work?" I suggested out of pity and curiosity.

Jim living in New York? My pride was dissolving fast.

"A drink sounds great. I'm staying at the Millennium. We can meet at the bar in the lobby," he said, still sounding like a zombie.

A few hours later, there I was again, at a hotel bar with this dashing but enigmatic man I kept stumbling upon.

The meeting with Executive Editor Howell Raines and company had not gone well. Every foreign and national correspondent knows the assignment comes with an expiration date of three to five years unless the powers-that-be bend the rules for you. These plum jobs—whether Los Angeles or Miami, Paris or Nairobi—are immensely coveted and rotational so that deserving writers all get their turn and the beats get fresh sets of eyes. But Jim's time to move on came up sooner than he'd expected when he got caught in the crosscurrents of the passing of the torch from *Times* executive editor Joe Lelyveld to Raines. As it turned out, Raines didn't last long. His tenure came crashing down twenty-one months after it began because of his autocratic style and a powerful trigger for the staff to push back against him—the scandal of deceit and plagiarism starring "the Fabricator."

Before he was booted out, Raines recalled many well-respected national bureau correspondents back to New York. Jim was among the correspondents who couldn't just pick up and return to New York as he had been ordered. Families can't be uprooted at a moment's notice and Jim, a devoted father, had two kids in California over whom he had joint custody. He had no recourse but to beg for his job. Jim was hoping that the new regime would appreciate that he had performed terrifically as a business reporter, a foreign correspondent in Asia, and a national correspondent in Los Angeles—most recently on high-profile stories such as the Wen Ho Lee spying case and the California energy crisis. He had won multiple Publisher's awards, an honor given to *Times* reporters who produced the best work of the month. Raines's predecessor had understood Jim's family situation and allowed him to remain longer than usual in Los Angeles. Jim thought he might be able to persuade Raines to do the same. But it was not to be. Jim would have to resign if he wanted to remain in L.A. After eighteen years with the paper, he was about to lose the job he loved.

He was devastated but had no time to wallow. He needed to find another job in the couple months the *Times* gave him to return to New York.

"It sucks that you have to find another job in a hurry," I told him as we sat in lounge chairs by the bar over glasses of wine. "Couldn't you move to New York for a while and take your time looking?"

I thought he was about to make a huge mistake. You can use the *Times* as a springboard to another great job probably only once. He could squander that chance as he rushed to line up new work.

"No. I really couldn't leave L.A., even for a few months."

I changed the subject. "Who hired you?"

The recollection of those early years cheered him up. Jim's ascent as a business writer was quick. In barely five years, he was sent to Tokyo to cover business and economics. He then went to Los Angeles as a business correspondent five and a half years later, before moving to the culture section, covering Hollywood, television, and the arts, and later national news as a West Coast correspondent.

For the next hour, we told tales back and forth about *Times* editors and laughed and gossiped. After a few drinks and two bowls of peanuts, we got hungry and Jim suggested Virgil's, a great BBQ place across the street. I wasn't about to eat messy ribs on our first "date."

"How about Orso?"

We walked to that staple of the theater district, and once there we found ourselves seated only a few tables away from the singer Lou Rawls, one of Jim's favorites. We talked and laughed some more, the mood and the feelings warm and relaxed. By the time we walked out of the restaurant, Jim was singing a Rawls standard, "Willow Weep for Me."

~./'~./'~Willooooooooow~./'~Weeeeep~./'~ for~./'~Meeeeeeeeee~./'~/'

He sang off-key on the sidewalk as I and passersby giggled. We strolled, very slowly, the two blocks to my subway station. We extended our good-byes until we had nothing else to do but look at each other awkwardly as people brushed past us into the subway entrance. Neither one of us invited the other to come home. That would have been too soon, at least for this lapsed Catholic. Then I remembered. "I'm going to be in Las Vegas in two weeks to run a relay race," I said as we shook hands.

It seemed my fate to always be headed his way. My friend in Long Beach, Rose, had roped me into joining her media team for the annual Baker to Vegas run through the desert between California and Nevada. And Vegas was just a one-hour hop from Los Angeles by plane. There I was again, serving myself up on a platter.

"I think I can find a story to do in Vegas while you're there," Jim said with a wicked look.

I smiled and said good-bye, but this time there was no fantasizing on my way home. My mother had raised no fool. I cautiously looked forward to our next meeting with no expectations whatsoever other than a nice dinner.

Over the next few days I pretended not to care that I had not heard from Jim, but, as the date for the Vegas trip approached, I couldn't help being annoyed. Here we go again. Jesus! What's wrong with this guy? The Monday before the trip, I finally shot him an e-mail.

"Hi, Jim. Hope you're well. My trip to Vegas is fast approaching and I need some suggestions. My needs, in order of importance: shops, swimming pool, blackjack, and anything else I can become addicted to in four days. Any help will be much appreciated."

Jerk.

He made me wait all of five minutes.

"We'll have to see what we can do about adding to the list of addictions, and the order," he replied. "Would you have dinner with me?"

Loved packing, loved flying, loved running in ninety-degree weather in a demented race involving more cars than runners, loved finally getting ready for our first official honest-to-goodness date. I was so nervous that nothing was getting done. With only fifteen minutes to spare before Jim was to show up, I still had to do my nails and iron my blouse. I was staying at the Monte Carlo Resort and Casino on the Strip. The room, shared with Rose and two other runners, came with an impressive view of the Eiffel Tower. My exhausted roommates planned to crash for the night, ordering in and watching videos while I was out on my hot date. They were so amused at my frantic preparations that one of them pushed me aside to finish ironing my see-through top while another one pointed the blow-dryer at my hands as I finished my manicure. When we heard the knock on the door my three roommates rushed to take their seats. Showtime! And there he was, showered and crisply dressed in a white cotton shirt and jeans, just off a plane and completely unfazed. He wore a big (sexy) smile and confidently (and sexily) walked into the room, saying hello to everyone while I blurted out introductions and apologized for not shaking his hand.

"I just did my nails," I said lamely.

He just kept looking at me, oblivious to my roommates and their winked approvals. That night, we dined in Santa Fe, strolled on the Brooklyn Bridge, and had pineapple vodkas in Red Square. Despite our fake world travels, everything between us felt natural and real. We spent hours talking about our lives. Jim and I shared a common background. We were both semireligious—not pious, but observant of traditions. We were both extremely close to our families. His mother, Levona, had died a few years earlier of lung cancer, but he still had his father, an engineer, and two brothers and a sister. He even grew up in hot and humid weather like I did, in his case in Florida, in one of the few Jewish families then living in Fort Lauderdale.

Jim had come to journalism in a roundabout way. As a restless teenager, he moved to Vermont for college and then spent a year in Europe, with his best buddy, Ken. They picked grapes in Provence, moved boxes in a wine cellar in Germany, and worked in a ski shop in the French Alps. After all that excitement he returned to the States to complete a bachelor's degree in philosophy and cultural anthropology at Middlebury College. He was foggy about what he wanted to do, until he got into the literature program at Middlebury's Bread Loaf campus and later the Bread Loaf program at Oxford University in England. He got the confidence to consider writing for a living and enrolled at Columbia's journalism school. Upon getting his master's, he lucked out. He landed an overnight-shift job writing and editing for the international wire service at AP/Dow Jones. Six months later, he was asked to open their Hong Kong bureau.

Jim had a girlfriend, whom he married, and they moved to Asia. The *Times* hired him less than four years later and brought him back to New York to cover Wall Street in the wild 1980s. He wrote a book about the collapse of E. F. Hutton, the venerable brokerage house, and went back to Asia to work for the *Times*'s Tokyo bureau. During his five and a half years in Japan, he and his wife adopted a girl, Arielle, and then a boy, Henry. Jim said he had always wanted to be a father. He was a natural. When I came along, he had already been divorced six years and was a self-sufficient single father who cooked, did laundry, coached softball, helped with homework, and worked as a national correspondent for the *Times* bureau in Los Angeles.

He had it all, almost. Like me, he was in a good place professionally but was missing a steady relationship. His dating record didn't seem to be any better than mine. While I dated insurance scammers, he went out with porn stars. Okay, one porn star. They attended a screening of *Boogie Nights*. For "research," he said, just to get an expert's opinion on the movie's accuracy in depicting the skin trade. The porn star—surprise!—showed up three-quarters naked, so, naturally, he took her to an outdoor restaurant on Sunset Boulevard where his date could stop traffic.

I laughed as he told the story over our pineapple vodkas at the Mandalay hotel in Vegas and felt completely at ease and happy. He said nothing about a crazy dog. We were having such a great time that when we tried to say good night we couldn't. I decided to live for the moment. But the next day, Jim had to work. We were up and running early in the morning, trying to make it to the Hoover Dam in time for Jim to report a news story about increased security at the dam, a popular tourist attraction, in the post-9/11 world. I wandered around as Jim interviewed visitors, some of them still visibly drunk from their gambling all-nighters, others killing time before their flights home. As I watched Jim taking notes, I was on a buzz of excitement and possibility. I wanted this man who looked and felt so right. It'd be tricky to get to know each other long-distance, but dating is never effortless. We could make it work if we wanted to pursue a relationship badly enough. And we did. We both realized that Vegas, hookup heaven, was the start of something more serious. We were so ready.

From then on, we sustained a bicoastal courtship. Phone calls every day. E-mails every few hours. Some were no more than symbols for kisses, deep as we were in lovey-doveydom. A few weeks after our Vegas reunion, Jim arrived at my apartment late one Friday night with a bottle of California chardonnay. I had a checkered past in the kitchen but welcomed him with a supper culled from recipes from *Gourmet* magazine. Prosciutto-wrapped asparagus with mint dressing. Grilled tuna salade Niçoise. Smoked salmon and egg salad sandwiches with capers. As we nibbled, we made plans for the two romantic days that lay ahead. He would take the red-eye back to L.A. Sunday night. My turn to visit would be up next in a few weeks. Arielle and Henry awaited.

It was all going to be perfect.

Five

The Big Galoot

arrived at Jim's town house in Los Angeles all frazzled. It was a hot summer evening, and I had just spent four hours crawling north from San Diego on the freeway. On that hellish Friday I had been attending, again, the National Association of Hispanic Journalists conference. The traffic was not the only thing making me sweat. I was about to meet Jim's gang for the first time.

Jim invited two good friends his kids liked, Angel and Michael, as buffers so the focus wouldn't all be on this new "friend." I had invited my own little security blanket too. Rose drove in half an hour from Long Beach. At his front door, I took an anxious breath, and pushed the doorbell. And there he was, my smiling boyfriend along with Greeter #2—the Barker. Jim had mentioned Eddie in passing so he wasn't a complete surprise. The dog seemed excited to see me, barking in a nonthreatening tone as Jim and I kissed chastely. At the touch of lips, Eddie jumped on his master, his big paws reaching to Jim's waist, seeking his attention.

"This is Mia. She's nice," Jim said, using the tone most of us reserve for toddlers.

Woof-woof-woof.

"You big galoot," Jim cooed as he held his pooch to keep him from leaping on my silk blouse.

"Hello, doggie," I said, careful not to touch him just in case he was overdue for a bath.

Eddie was covered in dark spots interrupted by a wide brown saddle wrapped around his muscular back and rump. He had a cute boxy face, but the spots were by far his most distinctive feature—not uniformly smallish spots like a Dalmatian's, but smallish, medium, and big patches, like a fabric print with defects. Any of his victims (more on this later) could easily pick him out in a lineup. He calmed down after a few seconds, took a few quick sniffs around me, and looked up at Jim for his next cue. A scratch-fest involving impressive contortion followed.

"What's a galoot?" I asked as the dog monopolized precious moments.

"A big tough guy," Jim said.

As he petted Eddie, the dog lay down and turned over with no sense of decorum to reveal a pink belly and God knows what else. With his four paws in the air, squirming from side to side as Jim rubbed away, Eddie didn't look so tough to me. I was relieved when Jim finally moved us on to the galoots that really mattered—Arielle and Henry. At eleven and nine, Jim's kids were still little, shy, polite, and monosyllabic to my questions. I felt as shy as they did under the circumstances. Everything was okay. The point of this visit was to familiarize ourselves with one another, to put faces to names. I hoped we'd have a lifetime to know one another. That night I had no expectations other than sheer success or utter failure. My friends' kids always said I was "cool." But winning over the children of the man you are falling in love with is fraught with danger. Would they be welcoming or would they be jealous? Would they help our budding relationship or try to torpedo it? Would they warm up easily or really make me work for it? I had no clue, mostly because loving from three thousand miles away shields you from everything except what the other person tells you. Jim was unflinchingly positive and cheerful about our bonding prospects.

Jim lived in a two-story town house he owned deep in a canyon in ritzy Pacific Palisades, home to the likes of Steven Spielberg, Kate Hudson, and Hilary Swank. His house was in the less glamorous area of the Palisades, in a neighborhood called the Highlands that could claim only singer John Mayer as its resident A-lister (and a visiting Jennifer Aniston when she later got involved with him). But Jim's cozy home was sun-soaked and inviting, and next to trails of the Topanga State Park system. It had space to spare compared to my eight-hundred-square-foot Manhattan apartment. Much of it was taken up by Arts and Crafts–style furniture and Japanese art and pottery that Jim had accumulated from his years in Asia. He also showed a fondness for some Japanese traditions. At his townhome, shoes were left at the entrance.

"It helps you unwind when you enter your home," he explained.

The place was neater than mine, very metrosexual. There was a high-ceilinged, roomy living room on the first level and a dining room overlooking the living area from a second level. Upstairs, the master bedroom was big enough to double as an office. Arielle's bedroom was upstairs, Henry's was off the kitchen near the dining room, and Eddie slept in a crate in the living room at street level. As the kids went off to do their thing and the adults chatted in the kitchen, Jim grilled some salmon on his postage stamp–sized patio and served it with asparagus and white rice—sticky, Japanese-style. I felt comfortable and relieved as that first evening proceeded harmoniously.

"He's such a great guy," my friend Rose whispered when we were alone in the kitchen. She was even happier that this romance could lead to my moving to California. That, of course, was where we were headed, since Jim was not as mobile as I was, but we were still in the getting-to-know-each-other phase. I had just met his kids and dog! My immersion in my boyfriend's life during the next couple days was remarkable for its ease. There was no miscommunication, no discovery of annoying habits, no surprises—although that dog was a bit peculiar. He wasn't exactly hostile, but he wasn't friendly either. If I called him, he wouldn't come. When he found his way to me out of boredom, he tolerated petting with no particular joy. There was no licking and only tepid tail wagging. The fireworks were strictly reserved for his master. For Jim, he jumped on hind legs and did the Mexican hat dance. He was usually confined to his crate in the living room when we left the house, so sometimes I'd do the honors of freeing him from his doggie prison. The thanks I got was a mad dash past me to Jim, who I could hear in some room talking his doggie-talk as he rubbed and scratched. I didn't see Eddie so besotted with anyone else, until one afternoon, when the doorbell rang and I answered.

"Hi. I'm Matilda's mom," an attractive blonde said by way of greeting.

Matilda, a mixed breed, mostly a Rhodesian ridgeback, was Eddie's companion on his daily walks by the creek nearby. I had heard a whole lot about Mattie, but not much about the tall and pretty thirtysomething woman who owned her and who now seemed to be studying me from head to toe. Mattie's mom wanted Jim to pick up her mail while she was out for a few days. I could not believe my eyes. Eddie almost knocked her down as he greeted her effusively, temporarily forgetting about Jim as he jumped up toward her ample bosom. He wagged his tail so hard his butt swung side to side. She seemed to have expected the reaction and bent over to scratch him as Jim introduced us.

Hmm.

"Did you date Matilda's mom?" I casually asked Jim later.

"No, she's just a neighbor. She picks up my mail when I'm away and I pick up hers."

"Are you sure? Because Eddie sure likes her."

"She gives him biscuits on our walks."

Okay.

Jim eventually fessed up to more than neighborly dealings. Apparently, at some point between the dog walking and mail exchanges, the two had been an item. So it seemed Eddie had made himself somewhat useful. At least he could raise red flags for me as I entered Jim's social circle. Good boy, Eddie.

The good vibes didn't last long. On a typically gorgeous Southern California Sunday afternoon, we all crammed into Jim's Volkswagen Passat station wagon and headed for Will Rogers Park ten minutes away. We hiked and played Frisbee. Eddie sat out the latter, since he wasn't a fetcher. Jim had once asked a dog trainer at the pet store how to get his dog to fetch.

"Oh, it's easy," the guy said. "Take something like a tennis ball and just put some gravy on it and let him get the ball and then call him back and he'll bring the ball back to you. He'll learn in no time."

Jim went home and slathered a tennis ball in some greasy leftovers and let Eddie sniff it. He went to the backyard and threw the ball. Eddie ate half of it and ripped the rest to shreds.

Eddie was a fighter, not a fetcher, as he promptly showed me. On our way back to the car, we came across a brown and black border collie wandering among the picnickers on a big lawn off-leash. We tried to scamper by, but the dog came at Eddie and Eddie at him. It was one of those scary growling moments. Cute Eddie was transformed into homicidal Eddie. Half his face had receded to bare an array of very yellow teeth and he didn't look so harmless—or attractive—anymore.

"Eddie, Eddie!" the kids called out in vain as the dogs squared off.

"Can you please put your dog on a leash?" Jim shouted at the owner as he grabbed Eddie and picked him up in his arms.

Really. There were dog signs everywhere. The guy gave Jim a fuck-you look, as if saying, "What kind of jerk are you that you think I need to follow the rules?"

"I'm just trying to walk my dog," Jim said. "Could you please restrain yours?"

"It's a Sunday. Chill out, dude," the guy said.

"Chill" and "dude" are not calming words. Jim started to get as flustered as his dog.

"Do you see what's going on? It will not be good. I'm just warning you."

"Oh, he's the nicest thing in the world."

At that point, somebody yelled, "Yeah, buddy! Put your dog on a leash!"

The guy finally grabbed his dog and turned to Jim. "He's got cancer! Leave him be!"

So much for Sunday relaxation.

We all went back to the car, with Eddie supposedly banished to the trunk area of the station wagon but managing to make his way to the front, past the kids, to pant next to Jim's ear and close enough to my own to make me cringe. His breath was like a gust from a warm oven, but it didn't exactly smell like croissants. Jim offered ice cream, and the kids focused on that. But I was focused on what had just happened. I wasn't thrilled that Jim had picked up Eddie in the middle of the brawl. What if the other dog attacked Jim too? I kept my mouth shut, but Mr. Fourlegs's family trips were numbered, as far as I was concerned.

Eddie wasn't finished. That same day, in the excitement of my first sleepover at his house, Jim forgot to put him in the crate after the kids went to their mom's for the night. The next morning we found him lying outside the bedroom door, next to a little wet yellow present. I later figured he peed because Jim had banned him from his bedroom at my request, even though Jim swore the dog never slept with him.

"He snores," he said by way of proof.

I didn't believe him. I found dog hair everywhere in the bedroom. Eddie was simply dismayed that I had taken his place. From what I could tell, Eddie in fact appeared to have the run of the house. He could lie on beds and sit on the sofa. He shed short, white pine needles that floated aimlessly throughout the house until landing on sweaters, shoes, even food. He had obviously soiled some spots where the carpet, never touched by dirty shoes, looked discolored.

As if I weren't disgusted enough, Eddie was allowed to lick the dishes and utensils as Jim loaded them into the dishwasher. It was something Jim's mother apparently had allowed Shayna, the family's rescue dog that looked like a big black Chihuahua, to do. Somehow it had become a custom passed on to younger generations. Even Hank, Jim's father, spoke of the licking ritual fondly. I found myself taking a deep breath every now and then. Don't be so fussy, girl. You've lived alone for far too long. Pick your battles. It's just a dog!

One night after dinner, Jim and I sat on the sofa, comfortable and romantic, having a glass of wine. All of a sudden, Eddie jumped on us as we were about to kiss. He put his wet snout between us, whimpering like someone had smacked him.

"Get back, back!" Jim shouted as I screamed, and he shoved him back down to the floor. I wiped my face with my hand and tried to regain my composure. Eddie plopped down by Jim's feet with a long whimper. It felt like he was throwing daggers my way. I was slightly spooked but also mightily bothered. Listen, galoot. There's a new sheriff in town and she ain't bearing biscuits.

I needed to gather some intelligence.

How did you two meet?"
Eddie's Cinderella story began with a father's promise to his daughter. She would get a dog when she turned ten, Jim's mom told Arielle and then told her son. Jim had no choice in the matter, but at least he could make sure the dog met a long list of qualifications. Not intimidating or hostile. Puppylike, energetic and fun. Preferably a female, maybe a twenty-pound terrier. Short-haired, so she wouldn't shed a lot. Responsive to basic commands. House-trained.

How in the world did this spotted beast get the job?

"And you got Eddie?"

"Well, our first stop was a rescue society whose only power in life is to deny people a dog. We went through this process, which was like getting into Harvard. They interviewed us, checked out our house. Every time there was a promising candidate I'd say, 'Fine, I'll take the dog.' But they kept saying, 'No, I don't know if this dog would suit you. No, it's not perfect for you. This dog isn't good with kids. This dog needs five hundred acres. This dog bites runners.' It was just ridiculous."

After several months of getting nowhere, Jim said, he found out about an end-of-the-line rescue place. They took in dead-end dogs. A woman, Jackie, rehabilitated them from all imaginable traumas and bad habits. Jim found himself in the woman's living room one afternoon as she presented her misfits.

"It was really a mixed bag," Jim said as he rubbed Eddie's back with a bare foot.

"There was Max, who was a miniature Doberman pinscher and the most hyper dog you have ever seen. He just ran around nonstop. He was definitely trouble. Then there was this big, incredibly intimidating pit bull named Brownie. That was the sweetest, nicest, most docile dog. He weighed about one hundred pounds. He was scary to look at. And he was completely dominated by this fifteen-pound Boston terrier named Molly. She pushed him around and kicked his ass. She was humping him even though she was a female, which is a sign of dominance. Brownie didn't realize he was one hundred pounds and could kill her in a second. I mean, this was a funny house."

Jim didn't find a match that day, but Jackie invited him back a couple weeks later, after she had inherited a new bunch of oddballs.

So there Jim sat as Jackie brought the dogs out one by one. One of them was fat. Another one was skinny. Tall. Short. There were plenty of cute dogs, Jim thought, but none of them seemed quite right.

"I wanted a short-haired dog and I wanted one that wasn't too big and I wanted one that had a sweet temperament, not too many neuroses."

Yes, we know. Picky, picky.

Finally, Jackie said, "All right. I think you're going to like this one."

"She opens the door and in bounds this spotted ball of love," Jim said. "And Eddie took one look at me and I think he just knew. He latched on to me and he was just not going to take no for an answer. He was on my lap. He was cuddly. He was sweet. He wagged his tail and his whole rear half wagged."

Yes, it's called finding a sucker.

"He was a little bigger than I wanted. He was a male and I wanted a female. But there was no doubt in his mind that he had found a home. I had virtually no say in the matter. I brought Arielle and Henry to see him a few days later and they really liked him. So we took him home."

"That's so sweet," I said. "How old was he?"

"Well, they thought he was about a year old, but it was just guess-work because he was found on the street in the San Fernando Valley, behind a dumpster. It was clear he had been abandoned. He was kind of mangy."

That made Eddie probably fourteen in dog years now. Great, a teenager. I smiled empathetically, looking at the "ball of love" napping. In his catatonic state, Eddie, indeed, seemed cuddly enough. I looked at Jim and . . . was that mist in my boyfriend's gorgeous blue eyes? It had obviously been love at first sight for him too.

But Eddie almost blew it. On his first visit to a dog park with his brand-new family, Jim let him off the leash to frolic and sniff around. All was well until Eddie spotted a pug puppy and mistook him for a ham sandwich. In no time the pug was halfway down Eddie's throat and would have died if Jim hadn't rushed over and successfully pried the nearly asphyxiated pug out of Eddie's dripping jaws. Arielle and Henry were hysterical. The pug's owners—two little kids with their mom—were traumatized. The mom, in typical California fashion, immediately threatened to sue. But her bouncy puppy showed a quick recovery right then and there, so this story had a happy ending for the pug, not for Eddie. The next day Jim took him back to Jackie and told her he couldn't deal with an aggressive dog. She promised intense rehab. One week of doggie boot camp later, Eddie returned for good.

Everything was peachy again in Eddieworld—except for no more dog parks for the mutt—until four months later. That's when I showed up.

I reached out for Jim's hand and kissed him. As Eddie snored softly, I had a feeling I would have much preferred Molly the dominatrix. I like smallish dogs that don't feel like a full-bodied roommate. And I don't like males that live to mark their territory. There was more in Eddie's unsavory past, as I would find out eventually. But it was easy to ignore Eddie in my blissful state with Jim. Our courtship continued to be nurtured by romantic reunions after monthlong absences and the growing conviction that we had found each other at exactly the right time in our lives.

Jim reluctantly left the *Times* and had no trouble landing his next job: national affairs correspondent for the *San Francisco Chronicle*, where he could work from home. The newsroom at the *Chronicle* now included my old friends from the *Examiner* after the competing staffs merged when the Hearst Corporation sold the *Examiner* and bought the *Chronicle* in 2000. I took the symmetry of Jim's and my paths as confirmation that we belonged together.

At the end of the year, I took Jim to Puerto Rico for New Year's Eve, to the house where I grew up and the neighborhood that remained frozen in time. The working-class El Comandante neighborhood near 65th Infantry Avenue, a main drag named after the segregated Puerto Rican Army regiment that served in American wars, was always sparkling this time of the year. Weeks before the holidays, walls and wrought-iron gates got a new coat of paint, front yards a trim. By December, façades were festooned with lights and lawns with Nativity scenes or Santa and his reindeer. The same neighbors always came out to greet me and comment on how *flaca* (skinny) or *llenita* (filled up) I looked compared to how I was the previous year. This time I had this handsome gringo by my side, causing much wonder and tongue-wagging. My parents, though, were long cured of surprises when it came to meeting my boyfriends. They had been down this road several times over the years with assorted beaus and had their hopes of marrying off their eldest dashed repeatedly. They welcomed Jim with ease and their usual hospitality, although my father had a look of amusement on his face, as if Jim were a friendly alien who had just descended from his spaceship and walked into the kitchen asking for directions to the beach.

"*Cómo está*, Rafael and Dinorah?" Jim asked my mom and dad in his memorized Spanish.

"Very good," said my mami in her memorized English, immediately planting a kiss on his cheek and hugging him.

Over the next few days, Jim got a kick out of what he thought were our funny customs and sayings, although he was horrified when I told him that New Year's Eve dinner would not be served until after midnight.

That night, as the kitchen bustled with preparations for the end-of-the-year family gathering, Jim's mouth watered with the smells of *arroz con gandules* and roasted pork, even if he didn't eat pork. (My mom cooked turkey for him.) As he hung out in the kitchen, Jim asked if he could help with anything and Mami handed him a clear plastic tree with spiky branches and a big jar of olives.

"This is an olive tree," she explained. "Put the olives in the tree." After twenty minutes of painstaking work (the spikes were too close to one another, Jim complained) he said "ready." But Mami gave him the tree back, pointing at all the branches he had missed. Welcome to the blunt, *sin pelos en la lengua* (outspoken, literally "no hair on one's tongue") Navarro gang!

As the party got going, my mom grabbed Jim's arm and showed off her daughter's boyfriend to curious relatives. The women kissed him on the cheek and my mom made him dance salsa and merengue with her. Jim went through the hazing good-naturedly. My sister found him good-looking and my father said: "I don't know what he's saying, but he looks like a man of character." Success.

Jim and I parted ways a few days later on Three Kings' Day, after watching a parade in Old San Juan with the Magi on camels. He left for Los Angeles, and I headed for freezing New York, to resume our separate lives and our longing for each other. Already in our forties, we were not wasting any time. I had kissed enough frogs to appreciate the prince before me. Jim was no fixer-upper. He met everything on my checklist. Self-confident. Kindhearted. Smart. Opens doors. Drinks without getting shitfaced. Not cheap. Good in bed. Holds his own financially. But more important, ours was that powerful chemistry that can't be described in words. My friend Bruce, then a theater critic and also single, used to tell me that what I needed was a divorcé with kids (since at my age I was unlikely to have kids of my own) who wanted to get it right the second time around. Jim was that and more. He was loving and dependable. He was sensitive and considerate. He wasn't afraid to tear up watching *The Kennedy Center Honors* or to talk about his feelings, sometimes through the existential stories of his favorite writer, Argentine Jorge Luis Borges. My soulful intellectual. When he got mad, the worst he did was sulk. He offered me a ready-made family. We shared the same values. He was only three years older than I was, but his maturity and self-assurance made me feel that I could relax for once, that I could trust.

And as a single father, he was house-trained. And he was hot! A dog? Give the guy extra points for "caring" and "nurturing."

Jim wanted me as badly as I wanted him. After his divorce, he had dated lawyers, television writers, agents, and other journalists, mostly in the entertainment world, but found no real soul connection. Like me, he had started to think he'd never find anyone. When we met in Arizona, he said he was struck by how loose it felt. By his New York visit, he had started to trust his gut. He said he liked that I was game, showed a passion for life and had a sense of adventure. He respected my trajectory from island to mainland. We had met up in Las Vegas not for a wild time but feeling it would be the beginning of a relationship. Very quickly, we both felt loving and loved. JetBlue, back then a start-up with cheap fares, facilitated frequent flying from JFK to Long Beach Airport, a throwback to the 1950s with an outdoors baggage claim next to the parking lot. Jim would pick me up and drive us to James' Beach, a late-night restaurant on Venice Beach, where the friendly owners, James and Daniel, served mahi-mahi tacos, sand dabs, and chocolate soufflé and let us sample their new wines, making us feel like family. When apart, Jim called me every night, his deep voice the last sound I heard before I drifted off to sleep. He sent me flowers so often the florist no longer had to ask for my name. He signed off e-mails with TQM, for *Te quiero mucho,* the essential Spanish learned from my nephews along with some cusswords.

"I'm sitting at my desk looking at a picture of a beaming couple standing arm in arm before a magnificent windswept beach," he wrote after our drive up the California coast. "What this picture really shows is a man smiling from deep within and the woman who inspires him with her happy confidence."

The kids seemed to accept me, though they clung to Jim when we were together. I was warming up to the idea of being a stepmom, although I wasn't fond of the term, which seemed so off the mark, with its negative connotations (thanks, Cinderella! You too, Snow White!). The Spanish word, *madrastra,* was worse. It sounded like a poisonous plant. But my ambivalence was not just about semantics. How do you relate to another woman's children as another mom, "step" or not, when the mother is both alive and very much involved? Do you strive to be more of an adult friend and mentor, like a favorite teacher or a best friend's mom, maybe? I didn't know other stepmoms I could grill for answers. I had to go with my instincts. My immediate priority was to not overreach or cause any conflict, especially between Jim and his children.

So far, my gradual entry was going smoothly. During an outing to Disneyland, Arielle and I were the only ones eager to ride Space Mountain. The minute we got into our seats, she grabbed my arm and didn't let go for the duration of the roller-coaster ride. It was sweet and eye-opening. I could love these kids, I realized. And I loved Jim even more for being their father.

I went camping in Big Sur for Jim. (Oh, yes, I did.) He went salsa dancing at the Village Vanguard for me. We spent a couple summer vacations with the whole Sterngold gang in Santa Barbara. Jim had two brothers, and all three siblings had two kids each of similar ages who got along swimmingly. There was also the sister, who was single, and the adorable patriarch, Hank, who kept calling me "a great gal." In his eighties, he played tennis, had a girlfriend, and was a total flirt.

I kept the romance under wraps at the office, since any whiff that I was serious about a boyfriend on the West Coast would have prompted speculation about my career plans among certain people. I had no career plans to speak of. I had not gotten that far. But like Jim before me, the time would come when I had to decide between the paper and my personal life. With no children or attachments other than my job, I'd have to be the one to move.

The *Times* was no small attachment. I had been a *Times* reporter for fifteen years, happily so. Unless the paper found a spot for me in California, I'd have to quit if I moved there. The thought depressed me. Moving to California also meant moving farther away from family again. I consoled myself, thinking at least I'd be creating my own family. But none of this was anybody's business at work, at least not yet. I was glad to have something else to occupy my mind: school. I enrolled in a mid-career program at Columbia University to finally get my master's in journalism. I'd need it if I ever wanted to teach full-time. Between my job, night classes, and long-distance romance, I was happily distracted, holding all major decision making temporarily at bay.

After more than a year of idyllic back-and-forth, Jim and I found ourselves strolling on the broad marble plaza at the Getty Museum on a warm evening, not far from his town house in the Palisades. We stood on top of a hill looking out on the ocean and the burning sunset, standing off to one side of a terrace. We were holding hands and Jim started talking about the day we met. He recalled that day in New York when he failed to keep his job and we went to Orso for dinner.

"What was particularly striking was how inauspicious that day was when we started."

I smiled and nodded, transfixed with the colors of the sky.

"I hadn't planned to ask you out to have a drink. I just was having this miserable day and ran into you because your desk was strategically positioned near the elevator. And you said 'Hi,' and suddenly having a drink seemed like a really good idea. And I ended the day singing."

~ . / ' ~ . / ' ~ W i l l o o o o o o o o o w ~ . / ' ~ W e e e e e p ~ . / ' ~ for~ . / '~Meeeeeeeeeee~ . / '~ / '

I laughed as he sang with his eyes closed, earnestly shaking his head. I also loved it when he did his Bob Dylan. Jim stopped singing and looked at me. On one of the worst days of his life, he said, I had made him sing. He was suddenly serious, even emotional. And nervous! I blanched. Was he about to propose? But he kept talking and I thought, Silly me.

Just as my excitement had dampened, Jim said: "There's no one else I'd rather spend my life with . . . Close your eyes."

I wasn't listening anymore as I opened my eyes and looked at the ring, a wide gold band with a large single diamond. I never thought I was a diamond girl until that moment. I couldn't get over the beauty of that ring and the perfection of the man bestowing it.

"Oh my God! Oh my God! Yes!"

I was happy, bewildered, euphoric. I was the same person, only totally different. I now inhabited a different plane, one with Jim by my side. I loved him so. We hugged and kissed for a long time with the Pacific in our sights, its vastness serving as a fitting metaphor for our future. Eventually we walked to the museum restaurant with views of the Santa Monica Mountains for dinner, but I could not take my eyes off my engagement ring throwing off brilliant rays of light from the candles.

That night in bed, I went from ecstasy to dread. Was I really ready for marriage—specifically, for the drastic transition to wife and step-mother, for the responsibility of other people's happiness? I quickly shoved the negative thoughts away. Of course I was. Jim and I were mature, intelligent adults. We could handle anything. He'd help me.

A more formal proposal came a few months later, when the next New Year's Eve rolled around and Jim and I flew to Puerto Rico so he could ask my father for my hand in marriage the old-fashioned way. I knew that over the years my poor parents worried that I'd forever be alone. No husband, no kids, just my pen and reporter's notebook. My father once—helpfully, he thought—suggested I fix a semi-crooked front tooth. I sometimes wondered if he thought I was a lesbian. But by now, my father had mellowed. For several years he had been deal-ing with cirrhosis and kidneys so battered he needed dialysis. He had been so sick that my mom held their fiftieth-anniversary party one year early, just in case.

But on this night of my visit with Jim, in the sit-in kitchen that served as the gathering point in the house and where my father sat in a favorite chair by the window, he was all smiles as Jim stood, nervous again, holding a piece of paper. My sister had put out chairs for herself, the kids, and a girlfriend, who happened to be visiting, to witness the occasion. They sat with giggles and smiles, waiting for this real-life telenovela moment. Jim's bilingual college buddy Alan had translated his presentation into Spanish and, with surprisingly good pronunciation, my fiancé made his intentions clear.

"I fell in love with a truly wonderful woman," he said, enunciating every word. "Each day I spend with her I feel like a winner at the racetrack."

Nice touch! My horse-gambling father was moved and couldn't give me away fast enough. Jim would forever remember the occasion as a scene from a Gabriel García Márquez novel—asking for my hand while half of Lorenzo Noa Street gathered to watch, unnerving him even as they enveloped him in congratulations and good wishes.

We still needed to figure out how we could be together, though. I halfheartedly looked around for other job possibilities on the West Coast, but I couldn't imagine not working for the *Times*. At the moment, I was covering sex and nightlife, a beat concocted out of the Metro desk's imagination. After so many years as a newswoman, I loved the change of pace and the challenge of trying to write about tawdry subjects without tawdriness. After all, my first front page story for the paper—the one I got on a metal plate from the printing plant per *Times* tradition—was about the "nuisance" of men "urinating in public."

Just as I was losing heart that the paper would accommodate me, the top editors cleared the way for my move. I was relieved and grateful when the paper transferred me to the L.A. bureau as the West Coast correspondent for the Sunday Styles section. At least my professional life would stay the course while my personal life shifted entirely.

Before my move, I went to Florida to report on the lingering phenomenon of Girls Gone Wild, the video series featuring college girls and young women inexplicably willing to flash their breasts on the street or the beach for the cameras. The story was pegged to the series' newer incarnation—Guys Gone Wild, which featured college boys and young guys baring their crotches. As I spent one night trailing cameramen through spring-break hotels and bars in Daytona Beach, my father went to the hospital in Puerto Rico in a catatonic state. Not long after I had gone to bed, my mom called with the grave news. He may not make it, she said. In a fog of sleeplessness and worry, I found a flight from Miami, and Bill, the publicist for GGW creator Joe Francis, drove me to the airport when it was still dark. He took care of my rental car as I rushed to catch my plane. One minute I was hanging out with naked drunks, the next I was racing death. Death won. My mom and her cousin Lydia were waiting for me when I stepped out of baggage claim, and they didn't have to say anything. My mom and I hugged and cried for Rafael Navarro Gonzalez, husband of fifty-one years, father and Korean War veteran, dead at seventy-six.

My father's long illnesses had given my mom, my sister, and me a chance to love him without recrimination. He was a different man sick and sober. My mom, especially, took solace in having sacrificed her quality of life doing everything she could to take care of him until the end. As for me, any leftover anger, any sense of shame, dissipated as if by magic the more vulnerable he became. His illness gave me a chance to get reacquainted with my real father. By the time my father left us, he and I had made our peace. After he died, all I felt was tenderness, all I could remember was the good. My father listening to Jim's proposal with a look of amusement and wonder in equal parts. My father joyously holding his newborn grandsons. My father driving me to my seven a.m. physics class at the University of Puerto Rico in his clunky blue Datsun. My father asking me to pick the horses in his *papeleta* during my trips home because he said I brought him luck. My father and I dancing salsa like pros at our extended family's house parties.

One day not long after we buried him in the family plot with his parents, a long-forgotten moment pushed forth. I was sitting on my father's lap as a little girl not yet old enough to read, listening to him read the *Blondie* comic strip in the newspaper. It was a Sunday ritual. I caught him making stuff up as a joke and told him to stop it in a scolding tone and to read the real thing. I kept a close eye on Dagwood and Blondie, who in the Spanish version were Lorenzo y Pepita, to make sure his words matched the drawings. And I caught him again fooling around! I protested until he finally gave up and read the words, which felt right but were not as satisfying as the belated love they would inspire decades later.

My sister and I initially worried about my mother, but she was eager to resume her life—as a woman in her seventies with a zest for a new, it's-all-about-me chapter. She traveled, she shopped, she hung out with Las Muchachas. And above all, she now could devote herself full-time to being a grandmother. My sister, by now separated from her husband, and her kids lived above our family house in their own apartment. My mother watched the kids after school, until my sister came home from work. With my dad gone, my mom was terrified of facing the nights alone. She bribed her grandsons with treats, whatever it took, so that one of them always stayed downstairs with her overnight.

I returned to the States to write about Joe Francis's soft-porn empire and to plan my move. Bill, the publicist with a heart, became a lifelong friend. Good-bye again, New York! Hello again, California!

Six

Evil Stepmother,
Here I Come

My move to California was relatively painless. Jim and I agreed that I should keep my apartment in New York, since we were certain we would end up back there at some point. My place—*our* place—would be an anchor. In the New York real estate market, once you're out, you're likely to be priced out when you come back and try to find similar digs. That's how I ended up on the upper tip of Manhattan after I came back from Miami in the late 1990s. Five years later, I couldn't afford to buy or rent in my old Upper West Side neighborhood. But Miami's dirt-cheap prices had allowed me to buy my first home—a condo on Biscayne Bay, overlooking South Beach—and I swore I'd never throw my money away on a monthly rental.

So to upstate Manhattan I went. I landed in historic Washington Heights, the area at the eastern end of the George Washington Bridge that connects the city to New Jersey. The highest point in all of Manhattan island, my neighborhood's hills were turned into forts during the American Revolutionary War. General George Washington lost the Battle of Fort Washington to the British just around the corner from our local Starbucks. Two and a half centuries later, the area was largely a mix of immigrants from the Dominican Republic and the descendants of earlier newcomers from Ireland, Eastern Europe, Germany, Puerto Rico, and Cuba, with contingents of Russian Jews and African Americans. I was able to buy what I didn't even know existed in the city for a single working girl—a financially doable one-bedroom with views of the Hudson River. The apartment and its gorgeous roof looked out to the Palisades cliffs on the other side of the river in New Jersey. It was within walking distance of two beautiful parks—the scenic Fort Washington Park and Fort Tryon Park, home to the Cloisters (the Met's medieval museum branch). Inevitably, gentrification would come and real estate agents would begin calling the area Hudson Heights to signal "upscale." There was no question I'd be priced out of my own place if I sold, so I found a colleague willing to take the apartment with her husband. A bit nervously, I left my one-bedroom with clanking pipes, holding a copy of *Landlording: A Handymanual for Scrupulous Landlords and Landladies Who Do It Themselves.*

In Los Angeles, I was adamant about getting our own place. This would be a fresh start for everyone, not just me. I didn't want to move into the town house, where I'd be disturbing the status quo. The dog had already declared me an intruder and I didn't want the kiddies following his lead. I found temporary quarters while we house hunted in Santa Monica, only a ten-minute drive on the Pacific Coast Highway from Jim's place. I could walk to the pier with the Ferris wheel and the Third Street Promenade, a pedestrian street with the feel of an open-air mall with restaurants, shops, and movie theaters.

I moved to California just in time for Arielle's bat mitzvah. Jim had been immersed in party planning and making sure she was ready after the rigors of studying the Torah, learning to read the Sabbath prayers for the Saturday-morning service, and writing a sermon about what her bat mitzvah meant to her. Is there anything more intimidating in the life of a thirteen-year-old? On the appointed day, I watched with admiration as she pulled it off beautifully in front of an audience of hundreds, including her school friends, family—many from out of town—and the congregation. In Hebrew! (Henry would be as successful in his own bar mitzvah two years later.) Jim was religious enough to raise his kids Jewish and light Shabbat candles on Friday evenings. I partook of the weekly ritual and had already celebrated Passover and the Jewish high holy days with his father and siblings. In L.A., Jim belonged to a Reconstructionist temple off Sunset Boulevard that was as beautiful as it was welcoming of this gentile woman.

As I settled into my new job, I mostly relied on Jim to look for our new home. As an avid walker, I didn't particularly enjoy driving. Los Angeles had walkable neighborhoods where a slice of pizza or a container of milk were only steps away, but we needed to stay in the Palisades, preferably in the Highlands, where Jim already lived, because of the kids' schools and a fifty-fifty custody arrangement. I'd have to drive for the milk and pizza. But where I lived was not a priority for me at that moment. The Palisades came with my strapping future husband, and that was all I cared about.

The Highlands was a planned community in upper Santa Ynez Canyon, surrounded by Topanga State Park. It was beautiful and quiet. About two miles up the canyon, it felt relaxing and separate from the cares of the city. We were definitely above the hustle and bustle of Los Angeles, and far, far away from New York. No more honking, sirens, train horns, and shouts of "Move it!"

"It's like going to the Hamptons," Jim said.

The houses were certainly almost as humongous and expensive. Jim was selling his charming town house for an absurd amount of money, so we could afford more absurd. As we looked at houses built in the 1970s, Jim was keeping his eyes peeled for nice office space. I focused on the backyard. I yearned for sun and fresh air and a yard big enough for dinners, for reading and sunbathing. As a bonus, the yard could also keep Eddie out of my hair. Maybe he'd like it well enough to stay outside most of the time?

"You can't leave dogs out in the canyon," Jim informed me. "Coyotes."

Oh.

It took a few months and a bidding war, but we found our love nest. I was pretty sure it would be the biggest home I'd ever have—a 1975, 3,200-square-foot house within walking distance of Jim's former town house. It was a typical California-style, open-plan, two-story house, L-shaped, around a small enclosed backyard with a lawn and a brick patio under a pergola covered with vines. The bedrooms and Jim's office—which would do double duty as a den/TV room—were upstairs. I planned to turn a downstairs bedroom into my office, and the family room off the kitchen would become a big dining room. It had a fireplace. I envisioned many happy dinners in that dining room.

A fireplace. A backyard. His-and-hers bathroom sinks. I had arrived!

One night before our move, we were in the kitchen in Jim's town house, where my adorable fiancé was seasoning chicken breasts with soy sauce to get them ready for the grill. I gently brought up some rules for our dog. As if his pampered life with Jim could get any better, Eddie would now have a full backyard to romp around.

"Honey, Eddie is going to have to be retrained. I don't want him in our bedroom or my office or on any of the furniture."

"Of course not. I'll take care of it."

"And I don't think it's a great idea to let him go in the backyard."

"No, no. I'll walk him just like I walk him now."

"Actually, while we get the new lawn he shouldn't go into the backyard at all. All he'll do is bring dirt into the house."

"Yep."

I loved this man so.

We moved into our new home on a Friday and spent the day directing movers and unpacking. The house looked great, with newly refinished hardwood floors and one wall in each room painted a pastel color, my Miami-influenced idea. After the movers cleared out, we brought the kids and the dog home. When we opened the front door—zoom!—Arielle and Henry ran up to their bedrooms as Eddie excitedly followed. For a while, all we heard was thump-thump-thump on the cream-colored carpet, even with bare feet and paws. Eddie discovered that the short, zigzag staircase to the bedrooms and den could be navigated in a nanosecond. He kept running upstairs and then downstairs, pausing just long enough for an obsessive sniff. Jim was somewhere outside, behind the garage, talking to neighbors, and I roamed around the huge space, stepping around the boxes, a bit disoriented, not exactly sure where to start or what to do.

Soon the kids opened the sliding door to the backyard to check it out, with Eddie on their heels. The kids lost interest the minute they stepped out, but lingered long enough for Eddie to get his paws coated in brown dirt. He tracked the dirt back indoors and left a train of paw prints on our new hardwood floors all the way to the carpet in the stairwell. When I saw the dog running amok with dirty paws inside *my* house, I was furious at Jim.

Where the hell was he? Didn't I ask him to keep the dog off the unfinished yard? Didn't I predict this? (It would be the first of my many psychic episodes as a married woman.) "EDDIIEE!" I screamed, grabbing him in mid-run so he stopped soiling the house. "JIIIIIIIIIIIIM!"

I waited for Jim, sitting next to his dog in a wrestling lock. We were both panting.

Was this new, beautiful dream house really my home? Were these kids and this mutt really part of my life now? Everything felt chaotic and out of control. Jim was my partner. He and I had to be a team for us to work, for me to feel supported in unfamiliar territory. Discuss, strike agreements, follow through. Yet here he was failing me on Day 1. Didn't he promise he'd make sure his dog didn't go into the backyard?

When Jim came in through the garage door into the dining room, his smile disappeared when he saw my angry face.

"This is exactly what I didn't want to happen," I said.

Without a word, Jim quickly took Eddie back to the garage to clean him up. My fiancé was surprised at my anger and didn't like it. He believed I was missing the point. This was the official start of our new life together. Why was I obsessing over the dog when we should have been savoring this happy milestone? Pizza arrived and we all gathered around the table in a nook off the kitchen. Jim chatted with the kids while I ate in silence and Eddie twisted on the professionally cleaned carpet, scratching his back.

By bedtime I had calmed down and started to feel guilty. I had overreacted. It was clear that I freaked out not about the dog but about my new circumstances. I had to take a deep breath and stop feeling so anxious. Could we rewind?

"I'm sorry I overreacted," I said when we were in bed.

"Let's make a promise," Jim said. "The Archbishop of Canterbury gave this advice to Prince Charles and Diana when they were married. He said, 'Don't go to bed angry.' I think that's great advice."

"Yes," I said, wholeheartedly committing to this beautifully unrealistic concept that not even Charles and Diana could follow under direct orders.

The next morning when I woke up, Jim was long gone from our bed. He was an early riser, even on Sundays. He had showered, walked Eddie, picked up *The New York Times* and the *Los Angeles Times* from our driveway, and served himself breakfast before I woke up to the chirp of birdies perched on the magnolia tree by our bedroom window. When I opened the bedroom door to go downstairs, there was a lump at my feet. Eddie was lying on the floor across the doorway. The first time he did this in Jim's old town house, I thought: How sweet. He's been waiting for me. But he wasn't just waiting. He was guarding me like a corrections officer at Sing Sing, making sure I didn't escape and attack Jim with kisses.

As I stepped over him, he sprang up and broke into growling barks. He barked as he raced ahead of me and escorted me down the stairs. He continued barking as I reached Jim, who was eating his usual cereal and toast while juggling the papers. Eddie was in hysterics, jumping on me, jumping on Jim, and trying to get in between us, preventing me from getting close enough to our man. Jim's solution was to give him a hand to lick. Gross. I planted one foot on Eddie's side and gave him a firm push. Out of my way, Eduardo. He's mine.

"Good morning, baby," I finally said.

Muah! I kissed him extra-loud to rise over the barking and perhaps induce such excited delirium the dog would drop dead.

"Good morning!" my sweetie said. "Did you sleep well, darling?"

"Very well, thank you. And you?"

Eddie positioned himself across the kitchen doorway, giving me an over-my-dead-body look. I had to step over him once again. All this jousting and it wasn't even ten a.m. I had to do something about this dog.

The dog was only one jarring aspect of my new life as a spoken-for woman. I was in a new time zone but lived three hours ahead, still on Eastern Standard Time, to keep up with the *Times*'s deadlines in New York. No more dragging myself out of bed at eight-thirty a.m. to make it to work at ten-ish. Now my home life superseded my social life. My immediate world consisted of Jim and work. No more staying up late hanging out with my revolving door of friends coming through the Big Apple. No more spur-of-the-moment whims, like rushing to the TKTS discount booth in Times Square just minutes before curtain to watch a Broadway show. No more me, me, me.

Now I had a car and lived in the suburbs. Now I had a husband-elect, two kids, and a dog. But I didn't miss New York, or "old me."

With L.A. and suburban life came a slower pace and different interests. I discovered the joys of hiking, which in L.A. came with the awe-inspiring payoff at the end—a view of the coast and the Pacific. In the consistently great weather of Los Angeles, we often grilled and ate outdoors.

In New York, so many things and people competed for my attention that I never had time for movies. But L.A. was a movie-industry town that I now covered as a reporter. Jim also had many friends connected to filmmaking. Sooner or later, the latest releases always crept up into conversation the way Fidel does in Miami or real estate in New York. I kept up. I took to L.A. easily, except for one rather disturbing pattern—in a predominantly Latino area, I too often found myself the only Hispanic in a social gathering who wasn't serving the meal. I made a point of making conversation in Spanish with "the help." I wasn't looking for a reward, but I always got the biggest shrimp.

In spite of the jealous dog—watching, watching, always watching—and our shaky start, I loved our new home and surrendered to its rhythms. I had a half-hour commute—enviable by L.A. freeway standards—on the Pacific Coast Highway and I-10. I passed the ocean every single day. Sometimes I made it back early enough to catch a dramatic sunset. A right on Sunset Boulevard, a left on Palisades Drive, two miles up the canyon, and I was home.

The house itself was an adjustment after apartment living. There was no super, no doorman, no co-op office with duplicate keys to make life easier. If anything broke, Jim tried to fix it or one of us had to stay home to let someone in, depending on what was going on with the workday. Eddie's job, meanwhile, was to go batshit at the stranger in the doorway and invite lawsuits. He hadn't taken a chunk out of any visiting human yet. His thing was more to intimidate, and he looked and sounded scary with that bark of his. But once petted by a visitor, he invariably calmed down and retired to the living room to pee on the carpet from all the excitement.

"What's that?" I asked Jim on one of our first nights home after getting into bed and hearing a noise above us.

"Squirrels," he lied.

We had rats in the attic. I'm not sure where Jim got the reference, but the exterminator who eventually showed up at our door wasted no time telling us Mick Fleetwood was a client. We feigned awe and let the guy set up rat traps with apple slices. The guy promised to be back in a few days.

"How long will it take to get rid of the rats?" I asked him on his way out.

"Hard to say. It gets hectic," Fleetwood Mac's exterminator said, waving his hands for emphasis.

Apparently, waging war on rats would take protracted battles and the signing of a peace treaty. He charged us two hundred dollars a month for coming by regularly to lay down traps and pick up casualties and wouldn't commit to a deadline to get the job done.

I smelled a rat.

"Doscientos pesos?!" my mother shouted on the phone when I told her about the scam. *"Que barbaridad."*

My mom, a handywoman who attempted to fix everything before calling for help as a last resort, offered to fly to L.A. to dispose of the vermin herself for that much money. No need. I wasn't fearless like my mom, but now I had a man in the house. After a few apples and dead rats, I shamed Jim into taking over the repugnant but straightforward job from Mr. Hectic.

Jim and I argued and disagreed over fastidious stuff as couples who live together inevitably do.

Me: "Can you please put the shoes in the coat closet? All those shoes in the foyer are unsightly."

He: "Can you please not put the knives in the dishwasher? It ruins the wooden handles."

Jim made fun of my meticulous coffee-making. Puerto Rico is a coffee-growing country and takes its coffee seriously. Its production is not big enough for widespread exporting, but I could make do in the States with any strong bean. I used an old-fashioned espresso maker set on the stove, and boiled whole milk, strained it of skin, and mixed it in with one spoonful of sugar. If the color wasn't exactly right— darker than lighter, but still more beige than brown—I kept pouring more coffee, then more milk, then more coffee—until I achieved the right hue.

"You're like a chemist in a lab," Jim teased me as I stood in my bathrobe, pouring away with both hands.

What did he know? He poured cold milk straight from the carton! Jim was not allowed to make my coffee.

Aside from minor irritations, Jim and I had to get on the same page about things big and small. My new Jewish family, it turned out, didn't eat pork. I first realized this glitch when Jim declined the traditional *pernil* on New Year's Eve in Puerto Rico. He occasionally ate bacon, so why not pork? That's what was allowed growing up, he told me. The restriction extended to the kids, which meant doing away with about two-thirds of my recipes. No pork chops with garlic, rosemary, and mustard. No pork ribs sautéed with eggplant. No pork roast in sweet wine. And no *pernil*, the garlicky pork shoulder served during the Christmas–New Year's Eve–Three Kings' Day holiday. I still cooked pork chops for myself every now and then, but felt a bit self-conscious filling up the kitchen with the garlicky aroma from the oven. I was grateful that Jim and the kids didn't seem to mind. In return, I ate their sticky rice. On the island, "sticky" means you've ruined the rice. Puerto Ricans cook it fluffy. My new family, however, preferred it in lumps, Japanese-style, and I got used to it.

More and more of the cooking fell to Jim, who spoiled us with his porcini pasta, grilled salmon with asparagus, and the kids' favorites, including ground-beef tacos, chili over rice, and plum cake just like his mom used to make it. On weekends, I made *arroz con pollo* or broiled spicy chicken wings.

Despite the culture clashes, Jim and I clicked as housemates. We got along, split the bills reasonably, and fell into chores instinctively. If he cooked, I did the dishes, and vice versa. If he did laundry, I folded. When in doubt, we had sex. Making plans, sharing love and life—married (or soon to be) life totally suited me. When we were (sort of) alone it felt like date nights, with candlelit dinners in our dining room and Eddie snoring away in a corner. But when we weren't, I had to learn to play nice. Now when he called out "Darling?" three heads turned.

The kids consumed most of Jim's time when they were with us. He was an extremely hands-on parent with homework, car-pooling, and playdates. He was so unlike my own father, who provided for the home but pretty much left the job of raising two daughters to my mom, down to the disciplining. If we did something he didn't like, if he didn't want us to go out, he'd send my mom in to deliver the message. It was as if he were scared of all that estrogen. In my new home, Jim and I tried to do things together—including dinner at the table, always—but the kids had their own social lives to attend to as they came and went between two households. Every Tuesday and Wednesday, and alternate weekends, they were with us. But they always had at least one weekend day with each parent, no matter what. That meant that on their mother's weekend, we didn't see them from Thursday to Saturday, but we had them Sunday night. When it was our weekend, they came back to us Friday and Saturday and went back to their mom late Sunday. My head was spinning, but everyone else seemed used to this. Eddie, unfortunately, never went anywhere.

My main job as a stepmom, it appeared, was just to be there. Jim basically wanted me to serve as a role model and supportive wife, not as co-parent. That was okay by me, inexperienced as I was at raising children. My involvement mostly entailed things such as going shopping with Arielle or showing up at school events to watch Henry read poetry or play the drums.

I tried not to be critical—not of the poetry, which was actually very good, but of behavior. I employed the three-strike rule to let little annoyances pass, speaking up only after three things had bothered me. Flip-flops discarded in the hallway? No sweat. Dining table left dirty after lunch? It could wait till dinner. Stomping upstairs? None of my business.

I tried to ignore the inconsequential stuff. I wanted to lavish affection and impart wisdom. I figured the children didn't need a third parent, so I didn't scold much. I knew the transitional first year would be hard on me, having lived alone for the previous two decades and having been actually fond of my solitude. What single woman has not looked forward to going home after work on a Friday night, changing into her jammies, ordering in Mexican food, opening a good bottle of wine, and settling down to watch a movie? Heaven.

I designated the master bedroom as my Zen space, a hideout with a dressing area and bathroom.

Arielle's bedroom was across from ours and her screams when fighting with her brother were hard to ignore. It was interesting how amusing this was when you watched sitcoms but how unamusing it became when it went on under your roof.

"Stop!" "Get out of my room!" "Daaaaad!"

I felt, strongly, that a harmonious household required ground rules. This was a matter for Jim and me to hash out. I didn't feel I could just deal directly with his kids. We had not bonded enough for me to start telling them what to do. I was also afraid of saying the wrong thing and screwing it up for Jim. My expectations would have to wait.

But I had no such qualms about the dog.

Eddie's hostility did not subside with cohabitation. In fact, it was just the opposite. He became more proprietary of Jim the more time they spent home alone. To clear his head during the workday, Jim took walks. Guess who the lucky dog was who joined him? Eddie sometimes got walked five times a day, depending on the news cycle. Then I came home and ruined his life. The dog greeted me barking with a craned neck as he sniffed around me and followed me as I dropped purse and backpack in my office and headed upstairs. By the time I reached Jim in his office, I was ready to kick the dog to the moon. What a pill.

In the new house, he was our undisciplined and untrained ball-and-chain. After we moved in, he quickly marked his territory with his butt, sitting on chairs, sofas, beds, and assorted soft surfaces, flagrantly ignoring his own doggie beds scattered around the house. In a matter of days, there was dog hair everywhere.

I had plans for Eddie, but first we had to bond. The dog was always there, ready for action, so a few weeks after we moved into our new home, I decided to go out for a walk with him.

How naive of me.

"You're going to walk Eddie?" Jim asked me in disbelief when he saw me grabbing the leash.

He had a look of both happiness and concern, much like his mutt, who was looking at me, then at Jim, as if watching a tennis match. At any moment, he would break into his *jarabe tapatío* Mexican dance and head for the garage door.

The business of walking a dog three times a day—much less waiting for him to select the perfect location to relieve himself and then picking up—was not for me. I never understood girlfriends of mine who swore their dog walks were their best way to meet men. How could sparks fly in such undignified circumstances? But here I was in sunny California, about to self-consciously pick up after a dog even after snagging the man.

"Yep. Might as well. Just want some fresh air. How does this leash go?"

The leash itself was nylon, but the part around his neck was a sliding chain that his rescue place had recommended because the harder the dog pulled the tighter it got, which made it easier to control the feisty one.

"Not so fast," my beloved said after showing me how to secure the chain around Eddie's collar and I turned to leave. Jim informed me that great danger awaited just outside our pastel-colored walls and sat me down for a briefing.

It turned out enemies lurked around every corner, through fences and behind gates. Jim instructed me to be in a state of constant high alert to fend off impending attacks. First, the coyotes. Jim reminded me of the stories we had heard about coyotes taking dogs off the leash in the area, usually little dogs. There was an open field at the end of our street and that's where they lived. Jim had a close call not long ago, when he was out with Eddie before sunset and he heard rustling in the field's brush. In a second, not fifteen feet away, a big coyote came walking out of the brush and confronted them. Eddie let out a wail.

"This was not a coyote who was just wandering around and stumbled upon us," Jim had told me when he came home spooked out of his mind. "This guy was hunting."

My resourceful fiancé had first stomped his foot thinking the coyote would take off. He didn't flinch. So Jim started backing up to the house without turning his back on the coyote. He was walking backward and pulling Eddie. After gaining some distance, Jim turned, scooped Eddie up in his arms, and started jogging, all the while praying the coyote wouldn't follow. The coyote jogged along with them but lost interest when Jim cleared the corner.

I wasn't sure picking up Eddie and running had been the wisest idea. "What if the coyote bit you trying to get to Eddie?"

"I wasn't going to be a sitting duck and let the damn coyote take my dog," Jim said vehemently. "That coyote meant business and his buddies may have been in the brush."

Jim stopped short of telling me what to do if I had a similar encounter. I think both of us knew that while I wouldn't go out of my way to feed Eddie to the coyote, if it came down to Eddie or me—well, let's not dwell on the unpleasant.

Coyotes aside, there was still the business of Eddie's foes in our extensive canine community. We were talking legions of them. Lest we forget, Eddie was a bellicose prick. In dribs and drabs, Jim had revealed his dog's rap sheet. Eddie once almost bit Jim's young niece,

Joanna. Eddie also got kicked out of the airport day care Jim used when he traveled for work because of fighting. And Eddie and Max, a golden retriever puppy from the neighborhood, had gotten into so many fights on the trail along the creek that Jim had to tie a yellow ribbon to the trail's entrance gate to signal to Max's owner that it was not safe to come in.

Like the father of the playground bully, Jim was always ready with excuses. Joanna annoyed Eddie by her play. Max was the attacker, always off-leash and always jumping from behind. "I'd go out of my way to keep my distance from Max, but one time I ran into Max off-leash by the creek," Jim had explained. "He took off after Eddie. They started to get into it and I grabbed each by the collar and pulled them apart. Another time Eddie was off-leash and Max again broke off his leash and attacked Eddie. I pulled them apart and the momentum pushed me into some bushes and I got scratched up and Max started biting on my hand. The wife finally got her dog and then blamed me. I said, 'Are you joking?' He was twice as big as Eddie. This was a dog they couldn't control. I can control Eddie."

The journalist in me suspected there was another side to this story. A certain Eddie-tries-to-eat-baby-pug incident in a dog park came to mind. But Jim was adamant that Max had traumatized Eddie and left him forever looking over his shoulder during walks, fearful of an ambush.

None of this exactly explained why the kennel expelled his darling dog. Jim complained that the staff conveniently overlooked Eddie's own injuries from the fights. The place separated dogs into big and small. First they put Eddie with the big dogs, but he kept getting into fights. The staff used water sprayers to break up fights, and they'd empty the entire bottle on Eddie and he wouldn't back off. Eddie sort of fell in between big and small, so they tried to put him with the little dogs next. They hoped the little dogs would be more submissive and that Eddie would behave. But he fought the little dogs too. He'd be fine for an hour or two and then turn on them. Eventually, Eddie ended up in solitary confinement. They put him in his own little caged area and it worked for almost a year, until Jim came to pick him up one Monday and they told him Eddie was expelled. At some point in the comings and goings of the kennel, Jim was told, Eddie had bit another dog around the neck and the risk of lethal injury had just become too high.

Jim still held his dog blameless.

"I got home and I was petting him and I felt these funny bumps on his ears and I saw scabs and bite marks," Jim told me. "His ears had been bitten through. Clearly some other dog had fought with him and gotten the better of him. It makes me think that the owner of the place had thrown Eddie out and made up the story about Eddie being the aggressor to try to prevent me from suing him for my dog being injured."

Sure. What logical person would not reach the same conclusion?

Jim was forced to board Eddie in a private house for a while. The caretaker had an old and amiable Irish setter. There's no need to repeat what happened. By the time I moved to California, Jim had been paying a babysitter to come and look after Eddie in his house when he was away.

Now, as I was about to venture out in the company of this thug, Jim warned me to stay far away from Pete, Max (yellow-ribbon Max), and Ally.

"Don't let the cute names fool you," he said. "These are ninjas in furry costumes." Never was I to try to pass them or even make eye contact with the owner, he said. I was responsible for smelling them before we saw them so we could cross the street or turn around and retreat. As he spoke, Jim was quickly scribbling. "Here," he said handing me a list.

Seattle. Golden Lab. Friend.
Chipper. Labradoodle. Friend.
Ally. Fat black Lab. Foe.
Pete. Ally's friend. Blond Lab, also very fat. Foe.
Chloe. Really pretty short-haired brown mutt. Friend.
Dancer, the whippet. Molly and Tigger, two goldens. All pals.
Casper. Golden retriever. Foe.
Max. Golden retriever. Archenemy.

"Watch out," Jim reminded me. "Eddie really has a bee in his bonnet about this one."

I think I was shaking a little by the time Eddie and I managed to finally leave. It was like entering doggie Mordor. With the leash in my tight grip, Eddie started with a swagger, like a cowboy out to collect a debt. We strolled our street, Avenida De Cortez, and it wasn't too bad. I discovered Eddie ate poop, apparently a delicacy for the refined palate of the cattle-herding blue heeler. He went for a turd left behind by a friend—or, more likely, a foe—but I pulled him away just in time.

We turned left from our house and right up the hill to the next block. Seattle waited behind a wrought-iron gate. Kisses all around.

Then sniff, sniff every blade of grass with identifying markers from other dogs, and we soon ran into some stranger, which was okay, Jim told me, as long as it was a girl or a geezer or a puppy. This one happened to be Buddy, a tiny terrier-looking thing with a mop of straight hair hiding his eyes. He was merrily lapping up water from the gutter with no owner in sight. I found a tag in all that hair and was able to track the owner to the house right in front of us before a coyote ate him. Buddy was a repeat escapee, the owner said apologetically. Eddie, anxious to resume his walk, couldn't care less about Buddy.

But down the same street, Eddie tensed up and started growling as we approached the house of a black and brown German shepherd lolling in the grass behind an iron gate that allowed him to view the front sidewalk. Jim had not mentioned this one, but there was obviously some serious bad blood. As we got close, the German shepherd threw himself against the gate with great force and Eddie battled against the leash, snarling. It was so bad I could almost hear them think.

"I'm going to rip your head off!"

"No, I'm going to rip your head off!"

The exchange was ferocious, but it was over in seconds. At some point Eddie grew bored and thrust his acrobatic rear leg into the air to let loose his most fragrant stream of urine on a nearby planter. The German shepherd went loco and I feared he'd impale himself on the gate as we walked away. Then, back on our street after circling the block, almost home free, our fearless hero made a totally dumb move and put his snout through the hole of a wooden fence so that two badass Pomeranians could bite him. I thought I'd be in trouble when I got home, but Jim totally understood. He knew his dog was basically a dumbass. But I felt sorry for Eddie later when I saw him curled up in one of his round beds, licking his wounded face. Every now and then he'd look up—giving me his "Do you have food for me?" pleading face—and I even felt affection.

I avoided dog walking like the plague after that experience, but sooner or later the time always came when Jim was not available, Arielle and Henry were not around, and it fell on me to take Eddie out. Then one day the inevitable happened. In Eddie's defense, the mail carrier drove his truck into a parking spot right in front of us as we minded our business on the sidewalk across from our house. What would Dum-dum be expected to do but lurch at the carrier through the open cab, bite a bundle of letters off his hands, and send paper straight into the wet gutter.

"Just go, just go," the mortified mail carrier told me, so off we went.

Then our mail stopped coming.

Apparently, thousands of carriers are bitten every year on their deliveries, forcing contrite dog owners nationwide to pick up their mail at the post office. In our case, no one was hurt, but the post office still made Jim sign some document giving assurances that we would contain our monster.

I became even more reluctant to walk Eddie after that incident. For bonding purposes, it was much easier to run with Eddie. The previous winter—the time of the year when the average Los Angeles temperature plunges to 68 degrees—Eddie had lounged around too much, even for him, and started looking like a sausage. Jim took him out for power walks and I decided to pitch in. Up and down the canyon we went jogging every other day or so, with no breaks for sniffing or getting in trouble. He soon looked more toned than I did.

But after several months, the dog still was not any more accepting of me. I pinned my hopes on Jim's upcoming trip for work. For the first time, I'd be all Eddie had for a few days.

"Woo, baby, woo," Jim said, confident that if I courted favor with his dog with scratches and biscuits I'd win him over. He kissed me good-bye and left me in charge.

I wasn't sure what to expect. The house was big enough for four of us not to run into one another for hours, at times. I thought Eddie would surely jump on one of the kids' beds and stay out of sight until I had to walk him. But the minute Jim left the house I couldn't shake the stinker. At first he took a nap by the garage door, convinced Jim would soon come back. But after a while, a bubble appeared over his head. It read: "Uh-oh." Alone with me, Eddie quickly transformed himself into a normal pet. He waited silently for me by the bedroom door in the morning. He clung to me all day long. We walked, we worked, we watched TV. There was no barking, no alligator stares. In reciprocity, I pet him and talked to him and left the kitchen's glass door open so he could sunbathe at will, even if I had to put aside my own fears of home invasion. The neighborhood was always teeming with gardeners, leaf blowers, painters, remodelers, cable installers, and taco trucks, but I locked up doors and windows as if Charles Manson were still on the loose. Just for this new, improved Eddie, I kept the kitchen's glass door open.

"We're in the midst of a breakthrough!" I reported back to Jim over the phone that night.

The next morning, I came down for my breakfast and let Eddie out in the backyard. "You do your thing, mister, and I'll do mine." I walked him after I ate and got back to my office to work. Not an hour went by before Eddie stopped by the doorway, looking intently at me. He looked kind of crazed. I ignored him, but he didn't move. I tried not to make eye contact. Still there. It was hard to concentrate.

"I just walked you. Go back to your tanning. Go! Scram!"

Eddie was going to have to adjust to me, not the other way around.

Somehow he was not getting the message. He left with a long whim-per at one point but was back at my door in less than half an hour. And after another half hour. And another.

I called Jim.

"Baby, Eddie is stalking me."

"You should walk him."

"I just did! After breakfast. His next walk is not due until after lunch."

"Well, I walk him whenever I go out for fresh air. It helps me think."

"I think just fine indoors. He'll have to wait. He has to fit my schedule, not the other way around. Do you want to talk to him? Maybe it'll calm him down."

"Sure."

I took the phone to Eddie's ear, and we both could hear Jim talk-ing nonsense ("You'll go out, don't worry"), but Eddie was not inter-ested. He was jumping in place, jerking his body as if we were about to set off on a sprint to the door. What a nag. I hung up, yelled at him "No!" and closed my office door.

Scratch-scratch-scratch.

That fingernails-on-chalkboard sound was the sound of me losing.

When Jim came home, I was relieved but satisfied that my rela-tionship with Eddie had been forever changed. But after rushing to greet my husband and getting his full dosage of ear and butt scratches, what did Eddie do? He turned to bark at me! By the time Jim approached to kiss me, the dog was in hysterics. Before Jim had a chance to bend down to calm him, I grabbed Eddie by the col-lar and threw him out in the backyard, slamming the glass door behind me.

"Where were we?" I said to Jim, leading him upstairs so we could greet each other in peace.

Jim eventually let Eddie in, and dog and master were once again inseparable. For the rest of the day, Eddie and I exchanged dirty looks. Life resumed as if I had not invested three days of goodwill on this double-crosser. I felt betrayed. The dog fooled me into thinking he had come around.

From then on, babysitting Eddie when Jim was away became just another periodic duty of keeping house, as mindless as cleaning up the oven. I would keep the dog alive, but that was about it.

The aggression, the walking, the hair—most dogs were just too much trouble. I had dogs, cats, Easter chickens, and rabbits growing up—and a cat that killed my rabbit—but as a grown woman, my life was too busy for a dog. It was just too much responsibility. And now all this inconvenience by association. Eddie brought unnecessary hassles to our already hectic lives. As far as I was concerned, he was a liability and a traitor. Inside the house, Eddie couldn't stand me, and only me. Did I mention the kids now insisted on taking turns sleeping with him? Of course, Eddie loved them! This was not the routine in Jim's town house. There, Eddie slept in the crate. Now, in the new house, the children needed him as a security blanket. Maybe it was a reaction to me. My fiancé figured there was no harm, dismissing my reminders that his dog ate "caca." The kids complained about waking up to Eddie's snoring, but they lovingly put up with it. One night, Arielle hosted him in her full-size bed. The next night, it was Henry's turn to cozy up to the dog in his twin bunk bed. I passed one of their bedrooms and there he was, sprawled on the mattress, giving me a ha-ha-I'm-in-the-bed-and-you-can't-do-nothing-about-it look while

Henry or Arielle sat at the computer. When the kids went to their mom's, Eddie had the beds to himself. He sometimes barked at the kids too, when they approached Jim, but he tolerated them much better than he tolerated me.

I scratched my head at this dog's charmed life. At some point between the Depression and the Housewives of Beverly Hills, Americans became dog crazy, and I feared that the madness had yet to even peak. Pictures with Santa at the mall for dogs. Health insurance for dogs. Fat farms and thousand-dollar motorized treadmills. Nanny services. Hotels with oversized pet pillows and plush doggie robes. Licensed dog masseuses. Yoga for dogs. Faux-mink coats, hipster lumberjack vests. And on and on. Enough to make one wonder how many carbon emissions American dogs contribute to global warming.

My perspective on dogs was an old-fashioned one, born out of growing up in Puerto Rico at a time when pets were treated like animals instead of family. My sister and I always had dogs, but our dogs lived in the backyard or on the terrace. We didn't walk them, nor did we sleep with them. We didn't buy them monogrammed sweaters or holiday presents. They were left behind when we went out. They did their business outside and were expected to fulfill their security guard job, scaring off would-be burglars. But even on the island, newspapers now ran "doggie socials" sections featuring pictures of dogs in front of birthday cakes.

I got it that dogs can be trained to do wondrous things. Dogs can stop fence jumpers at the White House and protect the President of the United States better than the Secret Service. And dogs can help us be less depressed, lower our blood pressure, reduce our risk of heart disease, reduce stress, and help prolong lives, as some scientific studies show. They even sometimes save our lives. Blake Edwards, the late movie director, said he once tried to commit suicide but his dog wouldn't let him.

But dogs can also make you run into oncoming traffic or fall on your face. And what if the dog was a constant aggravation? What does it do to your health to live with a dog who doesn't like you, who tries to trip you, who stresses you out? Where was the study about that?

Granted, Eddie was not as entitled as some other dogs. He wasn't ultra-pampered, that's for sure. A few days ago, Jim came home from a vet visit fuming. The vet had told him with great concern that Eddie's teeth were not cleaned and that if the teeth weren't clean this could start a chain reaction of illnesses and disease and Eddie could even die of a heart attack.

"Whaat?" I said distractedly as I put dishes away in the dishwasher. "What a crock."

"That's what I said," Jim said as he put some groceries away. "As if in colonial times they took their dogs to get their teeth cleaned or something? In addition, she told me that when they clean the dog's teeth they have to anesthetize him. So they put them under with an IV, which costs several hundred dollars, and then they clean the dog's teeth. I said, 'You gotta be kidding me. I don't think so.'"

"That's more expensive than it costs to get our teeth cleaned."

"And on top of it, they anesthetize the dog, which is a risk anyway. To make the dog unconscious?"

Eddie got teeth-cleaning edibles instead.

"They're much more expensive than regular biscuits," Jim said of some chewy treats called Greenies he found at Petco.

Did they do the job? No idea. But good call, hubby. There's a fine line between responsible dog ownership and crazy.

Eddie probably ranked five on a bad-dog scale of one to ten. He wasn't like my neighbor Karen's border collie, Hazel, who whimpered loudly until she got her way. Or my girlfriend Tammy's mutt, Sophie, who suffered from severe separation anxiety and couldn't be left alone in the house. Or my friend Robert's schnauzer, Christmas, who refused to eat dog food, have her wee-wee pad moved anywhere but the center of the living room, or wear a leash, and who had to be carried to the dog run. A two-pound speck of a dog could be as headstrong as a dog a hundred times his size, especially when wearing a bow.

But Eddie was still a big compromise for me.

Jim was oblivious as Eddie followed him everywhere around the house. He didn't notice the dog, but I noticed every disgusting thing. I saw Eddie scooting his butt against the carpet. I heard Eddie slurping his crotch. I smelled Eddie when I came into the house if he was due for a bath. I didn't want wet-sock smell in my house, so I became the bath scheduler. And I had to watch where I put everything, especially food. I tried to tread lightly, but things I had tolerated in Jim's place were less tolerable now that we were in our house. One evening I found Eddie all snuggled up between the armrests of my vintage chair upholstered in yellow velvet, and I lost it.

"BAD DOG! BAD DOG!" I screamed at him as I shook my index finger at his face.

I felt like picking him up and throwing him out the window, but he jumped out of the chair and ran away before I could grab him. I beat the chair's velvet like a conga drum, trying to rid it of dog hair. I turned the chair upside down, and that's how it stayed from then on when not in use by an actual human. I manically went around the house turning over other chairs, putting books and empty boxes on the sofa, and erecting barricades. Jim did not dare stop me. The house acquired a permanent just-moved-in look, but I didn't care. Who knew where those paws had been. Who knew what critters hid in that coat of hair. And I didn't want hair on my clothes or on the seat of my pants. It was not a good look. If I thought so, I would have been a yak farmer. I banned Eddie from our bedroom and my office, official hair-free zones except for my own hair, which, by the way, had started falling out at an alarmingly high rate since we moved. At least I could do my sit-ups and yoga on a clean carpet. Eddie learned to keep out even if the door to a banned area was open. I sat him down outside the doorway and said "No." I went into the room and he followed. I sat him down outside again and said no again—and again and again in a contest of hardheadedness. It took a lot of yelling and showing him out by the collar until he got it. It was six of one, half a dozen of the other to him, as long as he had company. He'd lie down by the doorway and doze off just like he would have inside the room. And Eddie could no longer lick the dishes in the dishwasher. Sorry. No. Too disgusting. With mostly instincts as my guide, I had Eduardo more or less under control in a short time. Wish it had been that easy with Jim and the kids.

Seven

Down Dog: Blending the Family

elax your facial muscles."

"Let your bones settle."

"Let your body sink into the floor."

"Melt into the earth."

Trying to melt, trying to melt. With every deep breath, I pushed negative thoughts away. Intransigent husband—swoosh! Indifferent stepkids, disobedient stepdog—swoosh, swoosh! Feelings of inadequacy—swoooooooooosssh! Melting, melting, pushing worries and faces away like clouds in the sky. Calm again.

I used yoga as a refuge. It centered me and kept me strong for my challenging new home life. After a few harrowing tries in New York—with tense yoga teachers, with one yoga teacher that allowed her dog to sniff our faces during poses, and men with disgusting toenails who snored during Savasana—I found the perfect yoga studio in the Palisades village across from a Starbucks. Quiet, relaxing, mostly women. The movie actress Jamie Lee Curtis, slim and nimble at an unidentifiable age, sometimes dropped in for added inspiration.

I needed yoga. Nobody told me that coming into an instant family was like coming into the game during the sixth inning. Jim and I, so in synch about so much, did not see eye to eye on how each of us could help blend our family. I was on "puree" but he preferred "chop." We shared plans as long as they were about the two of us. Jim and I—"us"—were in a different compartment than the kids. I often felt behind on what the kids were doing and where they were going with their father. The typical problem of planning schedules for kids was hard for me to follow or I wasn't always informed. Jim would forget to tell me about changes of plans.

And there were many, many plans. I entered a world of playdates and sleepaways, of tennis clinics and softball or baseball games and beach camp, of optometrists and orthodontists, of bar and bat mitzvahs, of drop-offs and pickups, of Timmys and Jesses. Everything required a high level of coordination. After Jim coordinated with the ex and the children, he was at times too distracted or exhausted to pass along the many details to me. He shielded me from the ex, which I appreciated, and from most of the work, which I wished he hadn't. He arranged playdates and the doctors' appointments. He did most of the cooking and the driving. He tried to make it all work. More often than not, he also managed to be Super-husband-elect. Mere mortal me felt a little frustrated, a little in the way. I didn't do much for the children. It was hard to know when to step in or step back.

Sometimes it was the little things.

"We're going to Malibu Country Mart and would love it if you could join us," Jim chirped on Saturday morning as I was getting up.

That was too much action for me before my first cup of coffee. "Oh, no, go right ahead. Have fun," I said.

A little notice would have been nice. I slept in on weekends, true, and Jim and the kids were up early, but I felt it would have been great if we had gone through the day's plans together, even if the plans were improvised. Eddie was also left behind. The dog and I kept each other company for the next lazy hours, all the while wishing we were in Malibu too.

I understood that Jim was in the middle of many pressures. And none of this stopped me from falling more in love. But there was a sticking point. Jim had an enormous capacity to empathize with his kids when they acted up. He looked for the reasons behind the misbehavior, the anger. He listened, he reassured. He offered drinks and popsicles. He subscribed to the let's-keep-them-hydrated school of discipline. I was a product of the another-word-and-you're-dead parenting system.

You know how some parents encourage outspokenness, strong-mindedness, even rebelliousness, all in the name of nurturing individualism? Well, that's not the Latin way. Where I grew up, parents constantly kissed and hugged their children, but they turned to stone before you could say "Just kidding!" the minute they heard any lip. Latin American parents take pride in kids being respectful and "well educated," meaning not that they went to Harvard but that they are polite. The word for those who stray is a *malcriado*, or "badly raised." A *malcriado* is walking evidence of bad parenting. Where I grew up, adults did not nurture individualism as much as they demanded humility, respect for authority, loyalty to the family, deference to elders, good manners, and obedience. You asked them for their blessing—*bendición*—by way of hello and good-bye. Really, Latin parents would have been unbearable had they not been so hip. They pierced our newborn ears and let us drink coffee while we were still playing with Barbies. (I liked my coffee before school piping hot, with cubes of melted cheese inside. Yum-yum.)

"Get up. Leave your seat to the *comadre*."

"Go get me my purse."

"*Pórtate bien*. Behave."

"Don't be ungrateful."

That was the soundtrack of my childhood. You'd say something like "Who cares?" at your own peril. My mother's head would have spun like Linda Blair's in *The Exorcist* and I'd still be hiding in the bathroom. "I hate you"? Silly, silly you for thinking that would even be possible. An ill-timed shrug or door slam could send my mommy into a rage and in search of the flyswatter—"Go get me the flyswatter!"—to beat on my legs. I just felt little pricks but faked great hurt—Waaaaaaaaaaah!—much like a fouled basketball player. I could play this game too. But I also knew my dear mami had zero tolerance for crap or drama. She worked too hard for that. She was always coming and going—to work, to the supermarket, to school—always busy, busy.

In her preschool years, my sister stayed with our maternal grandmother during the workweek so my mom could deal. I was dropped off after school at a friend's—Maria Esther, my friend Diana's mother and one of the stay-at-home Muchachas in my mom's circle of girlfriends. I was with Maria Esther the day President Kennedy was shot. Maria Esther had dropped her wallet in a puddle and I was helping her hang wet dollar bills from a clothesline in the backyard when the next-door neighbor came running to us, screaming the news. For a while, Diana's family lived on the sprawling second floor of an old house near our school, next to a funeral home. Our favorite pastime was to huddle by a window and wait for the hearse to deliver the latest *muerto* and try to catch a glimpse of the corpse. If we were lucky, the feet would show as they took the body out, at which point Diana, her younger brother, and I would bolt from the window screaming and then have horrible nightmares at night. By the age of about twelve I was old enough to be a latchkey kid and take care of myself and my sister after school. And did I relish that role. From about two to five p.m., I had my sister, who was four years younger, all to myself to boss around.

"Go do your homework."

"Go shower."

"Get me some milk with Quik."

I loved the power. Looking back, I realized I was also getting even. I was jealous when my sister came along and sucked up all the air. My jealousy was my mom's fault more than my innocent baby sister's, but I wasn't that clearheaded as a four-year-old. From the moment my sister was born, I felt my mom devoted all her attention and sweet nothings to that cute blob. As we grew up, she could do no wrong.

"You're the oldest, you should know better," my mom repeated after every sibling fight or disagreement.

It was terribly unfair and I had no choice but to try to kill my sister. I was five or so. She was in her crib, standing up unsteadily while holding on to the railing. I was in front of her when the railing came down and she tumbled out. I didn't remember consciously trying to harm her. But how did she fall? Sheepishly, I went to the kitchen to find my mom, and stood there for a few seconds watching her cook, and finally said: "*La nena se escocotó.*" My mom rushed to the bedroom and found my sister unconscious on the floor. She screamed, she cried, she asked me what happened. It was like a scene from *The Bad Seed*. I didn't mean it.

My dear sister survived and grew up to be the mother of three well-behaved young men. We disagreed about many things, but not about how children should be raised. We recognized some of the excesses of our upbringing—in my case, my mother didn't think twice about violating my privacy. I caught her once reading my correspondence when she came to visit me in Washington. We both pretended it was normal and neither one said a word, but I hid the letters better going forward. I knew she didn't see anything wrong with it, just like I could walk in on her in the bathroom to put on mascara and she didn't mind it a bit. I had come out of her loins. There was no such thing as having your own "space." But I had lived in the States long enough to identify and appreciate a balance in parenting styles. I had watched some of my childhood friends raise their own American kids. I was confident in the Rican method and how to modify it to suit a more free-form parenting style.

I was utterly unprepared, though, for the day I heard Henry curse at his father. I almost had a conniption. While my eyes popped out of my head and my hands trembled, Jim followed Henry to his room so they could talk it over. Jim sought understanding, and they were good with each other in no time. It wasn't my way. I would have talked it out but also imposed consequences. Cursing? At a parent? A minimum of house arrest in an orange jumpsuit.

A few days later, I called my mom. She was sniffling.

"Do you have a cold?"

"No. It's Lucero. She just lost the baby."

"Who?" I asked, alarmed.

Then I heard the TV in the background and realized she was watching her favorite telenovela.

"Give her my condolences," I told Mami. "Can you tape the show? I got my own telenovela on. You wouldn't believe what goes on in this house. The tail wags the dog. Oh, and the real dog hates me."

"Leave the kids to Jim," she said. "Stay out of it."

What? Who was this woman?

Jim agreed with my mom. I knew he worried that asserting myself too soon could affect my efforts to build a relationship with the children. But this was all kiddie stuff, I thought. Fighting, screaming, letting out bad language here and there? From my vantage point, parents had so many more options these days to assert themselves—"or else"—with all those computers, video games, and gadgets to pry out of little hands.

I gingerly ventured in from the sidelines.

"Baby, I think Arielle and Henry need to know there will be consequences when they disrespect you or act mean toward each other. It's great that they always apologize afterward, but the behavior is repeated way too often."

Jim was quick to defend his children. He offered many reasons to explain their bad moods. He was not taking to my feedback as warmly as I had expected. I pressed on.

"If they start screaming, why don't you at least tell them that that's unacceptable?"

"I tell them when something's wrong, but I want them to know I will listen to them. I share your goals, darling."

I was proud of us. This was the kind of communication couples needed to make a marriage work. You discuss, you reach consensus, you follow up.

But Jim didn't respond as I'd hoped. He was often concerned about needlessly turning something small into something big. He believed empathy could solve many disciplinary problems.

I loved my husband, but I was convinced there was something off about his views. I wondered, did this stem from guilt over the divorce? Competition with the ex for most popular parent, for custody of a child's love? Something in his own upbringing? He would have never taken raised voices from anyone else. Did he feel this was just a phase?

One night, when I'd had enough, I went into Henry's room as he was yelling and I tried to intervene. But Jim intercepted me. He said he could handle it and didn't want to make Henry even more upset. I was hurt, but I retreated without a word. In our bedroom, I lay down fuming but trying to understand why Jim and I seemed stuck in conflict over child-rearing. Was it a Taurus–Libra thing? (Guess who sought compromise and who charged like a bull.) I admitted that I was very black-and-white, and that it was easier for me to be less emotional about children who were not mine. But we needed to reach some form of consensus and stick to the plan. I worried that the disrespect would soon spill over onto me. Time was flying. Oncoming teenagers! We grown-ups needed to unite.

The kids behaved much better when their dad was not around (sound familiar?). So far both Arielle and Henry had been warm toward me. And they loved Eddie. They walked him, they scratched him, they talked to him, they slept with him. Henry was artistic and liked to spray-paint and write poems. He spent hours in the garage making beautiful graffiti art. Jim got him cans of paint and very large rolls of wide paper so Henry could paint long graffiti murals, about eight to ten feet long and four feet high. They were basically bubble-lettered slogans and nicknames, rather joyfully colored, with designs in the background and over the words. He made me birthday cards with drawings of little hearts and "Happy B-day Mia" in graffiti letters. He had talent and was starting to make designs for T-shirts he hoped to sell online. Arielle was a good student and a fierce tennis player. Both had many friends from school and from the neighborhood, so many, in fact, that they were hard to keep track of in conversation. I was always asking Jim to catch me up.

"Is Stevie the one who drives the Corvette on his dad's lap?"

Henry was very much his daddy's boy and we didn't hang out as much as Arielle and I did. My stepdaughter and I enjoyed going to the Santa Monica mall or on special outings such as a night at the ballet. We talked easily over lunch and she was quick to apologize for any minor transgression. I so wanted for all of us to be at ease with each other. What did I know about raising kids other than my mother's example? It was a different world today and my stepfamily was an unconventional one by several layers. I decided I needed to hit the books. I had gone online and spent a small fortune on a survival library of stepparenting self-help books. Now was the time to open them. The first one, *Encouraging Words for New Stepmothers*, didn't disappoint.

"The situation is crazy. Not you."

Thank you.

"The situation" was no piece of cake for the children or the husband either, the book noted. "In the first couple of years everyone is likely having a hard time adjusting."

First couple years? *Encouraging Words* was sounding less encouraging. It couldn't possibly take that long. But as I read this and other books, I found out that it can take as long as seven years for the members of a stepfamily to fully integrate. Children often cling to the hope that their parents will get back together.

I turned to *Making It as a Stepparent*, which warned that children and money, "in that order," were the most often cited reasons in the breakup of second marriages. Not that stepparents and stepchildren couldn't discover friendship and enrich each other's lives, said the author. But initially, you may resent your instant children and feel jealous of them—and of your husband for being their parent. You may not even like his kids, the author noted. Whoa. I had not even thought of that. Maybe I should stop reading and not add to my worries. But I couldn't put the books down. They spoke to me like a friend who knew all my secrets—even the ones I didn't know I had. I skipped to the chapter on discipline and found myself in more familiar territory. Whatever the discord, the book said, the couple must present a united front.

Yes!

"When they sense there's disagreement, children will play one parent off against the other."

Of course! I didn't need a book to tell me that. We had all done that to our own parents. The author advised to fully participate in childrearing and disciplining stepchildren, but to build rapport first.

I wondered if Jim would allow my full participation. One thing was to change his style, another to let me impart discipline.

"The issue must be faced," the book warned. "Is the real parent prepared to share his children?"

Good question.

Jim and I never talked about this in such specific terms. We were both newbies at this. But why would he want to bring me into his family if he wasn't prepared to share responsibilities? We loved, respected, and admired each other. We trusted each other's judgment. We were rational people. We'd make our own rules and work it all out. I didn't doubt it for a second. We'd get this discipline issue out of the way so I could be free to become only one kind of stepmother—the cool one. When Christmas rolled around, I got a big tree, the kind I could have never fit into my New York apartment. My Jewish stepkids loved it and helped decorate it. I had less success with my "chores board." I gathered my family around one Saturday and showed the kids how they could help out on their days with us. Little things like cleaning the table after dinner, putting dishes away in the dishwasher, taking clean dishes out of the dishwasher—all jotted down on an erase board by day of the week. Father, daughter, and son all nodded in agreement and smiled as if saying "Isn't she cute?" Some chores got done—others didn't—whenever anyone remembered, despite my carefully laid-out schedule.

But I had absolutely no doubt I would marry my prince. No misgivings whatsoever. Jim was my cocoon of love and support. We were perfect for each other and cherished our time together. We hiked to the Eagle Rock summit in the Santa Monica Mountains and jogged along the ocean off the Pacific Coast Highway in always sunny L.A. (No bathing in the cold, polluted waters, though. This wasn't Puerto Rico's Luquillo Beach.) We took spur-of-the-moment day trips. One morning we got in the car and headed for Los Olivos in Santa Ynez Valley, our closest wine region, not even three hours away. We wanted to eat grilled artichokes and quail at the Hitching Post and drink the restaurant's own pinot noir, later made famous by the movie *Sideways*. Santa Ynez was not overrun by tourists like Napa Valley. It had its own grand wineries, such as Firestone, but the region was more low-key rural, with smaller wineries such as Sanford and Blackjack Ranch in Santa Barbara County.

Jim also wanted to drop in on Bob Senn. Bob had this lovely little wine store, Los Olivos Wines & Spirits Emporium, outside of town. Jim had met Bob while doing a story for the *Times* about the endangered California tiger salamander, which lived underground almost the entire year and came out to mate when it was really windy, rainy, and sucky in the spring and pools collected at the bottom of the hills. There was a movement under way to stop the wineries from ripping out the old California oaks and blanketing the hills with vineyards, killing off the places where the salamanders mated. Bob Senn was one of the characters Jim met in the town when reporting the story. They became fast friends.

His shop looked more hardware store than emporium, with Jim's story on the salamander framed and hung on a wall. Bob greeted us like old friends and started pouring. He had interesting new wines. We chatted and sipped and bought wine and drank some more. Another couple joined us, and we shared more drinks. They mentioned they were both L.A. sheriff's deputies on their day off. We drank to that too. At some point, we said our good-byes and stepped out into the dusk. Outside the store, we realized we couldn't go anywhere. We were wasted and two sheriff's officers had just seen us leave. We were stuck. Unable to drive—and afraid we'd be arrested for DUI—we had to wait more than an hour until the deputies left. But we didn't care. We opened the back of Jim's station wagon and sat there making out like two teenagers.

Back to L.A. and sobriety, there was a wedding to plan. I, frankly, wanted to elope. "Just you and me in Vegas again," I told my sweetie, who was tempted. But he clearly preferred a family affair and he knew I ultimately did too. We would cherish the memories. We wanted to share our good fortune. I succumbed to planning a traditional wedding also for my mother's sake. It had been a year since my father's death and we were all eager for a reunion, a joyous one, with family and friends. Since even a house party in Puerto Rico required dancing, Jim enrolled in merengue and salsa dance lessons. Merengue is like marching in place, only sensual, and much easier to learn than salsa. Jim mastered the rhythm in no time.

"Remember—mar-ching, mar-ching," I instructed as we practiced at night in the kitchen.

Our brilliant dog couldn't take the dancing. Maybe he thought we were fighting. Every time we came together in the dance hold and marched in place, Eddie got all upset and started running circles around us, jumping on us and biting Jim's Bermuda shorts as he tried to pull us apart. "Look, Eddie—me-rrrren-gue!" Jim said as he kept counting steps and mar-ching, mar-ching to the beat.

Jim was joking around, but I was on high alert. If the dog thought we were fighting, I wasn't the one he was going to protect. Although Eddie's behavior as protector was, to put it mildly, erratic. Yes, he almost bit the mail carrier. But this was how Eddie guarded me inside our home one afternoon: A noise downstairs signaled a potential break-in. I was upstairs in the den, with Eddie buried in his round cushion, dreaming of rabbits, and I was not going to get up to check around because I happened to be engrossed in a *Law & Order* episode I had taped a month and a half earlier and finally got a chance to watch. In any event, going downstairs to investigate a possible threat was Eddie's job. But minutes went by before he woke up to the persistent noise. As a possible homicidal maniac continued to lurk, our home security system stirred. His eyes froze in a vigilant stance. He growled from deep within, building up to a few hiccups of a bark. He vibrated with the effort but remained immobile in his doggie bed. The noise died down and so did the vigilance of our guard dog, who went back to chasing rabbits. Honestly, Eddie showed much better ability as a vacuum cleaner.

Now, as we practiced our merengue dance, Eddie's hissy fit—prompted by frustration that he was the dog and I was the bride, no doubt—got louder and I caught Jim offering him a hand to lick behind my back.

I had to laugh. "Stop cheating on me!"

After all that marching in place and all those checks on the interminable wedding to-do list, Jim and I were married in Puerto Rico before a judge because we couldn't find a priest to forgive Jim's divorce. We searched and searched, but the Catholic Church didn't approve of our marriage. One priest even suggested an annulment of Jim's first marriage—in fifty easy steps! The church didn't manage to dampen our mood, even though my mom, a devoted churchgoer, was disappointed. But we held the wedding in a former convent, so that counted for something. Hotel El Convento in Old San Juan had a lush Spanish-style courtyard, where we held the ceremony and cocktails, and an air-conditioned salon for dinner and dancing. In attendance were seventy-five relatives and friends who had seen me grow up—cousins and uncles and aunts and a few of my childhood friends—and also friends from the States. My cousin Alma, a soulmate who is more like a big sister than a cousin, even though I called her Titi, or Auntie, was my maid of honor, and my younger sister was my bridesmaid, along with Arielle; two girlfriends from kindergarten, Diana and Celia; and Edna, my buddy from New York. Titi Alma was in

her fifties but had the onset of Alzheimer's and seemed a little confused by the goings-on. Jim's brother Paul was the best man. Henry
got along swimmingly with my youngest nephew, Alexander, and the
two were inseparable through ceremony and reception. Hank, my
brand-new father-in-law, danced with my mother and pretty much
everyone else. The families merged easily. Jim and I were happy-
happy, even though the hotel misspelled Sterngold on the welcome
sign in the lobby and Jim barely understood the judge's English.

"Are we really married?" he joked after the ceremony.

"Yeah, Mr. Navarro!" (I kept my maiden newspaper byline.)

Jim and I got married nearly four years after our first encounter at
the bar in Phoenix. We had survived a long-distance relationship of
almost two years before I moved to California and we were finally
able to create our home. Our love had prevailed despite the distance
and the odds. We had done it!

It did feel different to be married, I thought as we walked outside to have our photos taken on the blue cobblestone streets of Old
San Juan. Love felt more proprietary, on a more stable footing. Jim
later delivered a toast in his limited Spanish, which everyone appreciated, and we did our merengue, which further impressed the crowd.
We added a couple arm flourishes and the room went wild. A cousin
known for his bootleg rum flavored with guava, tamarind, and other
tropical fruits regaled us with a slightly out-of-tune a cappella song.
My mami was ecstatic, even as she, my sister, and I missed Papi terribly. My sister cried throughout the ceremony, thinking of him. But
my mom was mostly relieved. She had lived to see her oldest marry—
finally!—a good man she fondly called her "favorite gringo." Mami,
who nervously walked me down the aisle to my groom, after my
nephews, Jonathan and Miguel Angel, walked me to her, once told my

sister she worried about dying while I was still single. "She's all alone," she said. My wedding was her crowning achievement.

After a lovely four-day honeymoon on Tortola, where there was nothing to do but make love and drink rum (and, in my case, get seasick snorkeling), my brand-new husband and I came home to plan the second phase of our wedding—a Jewish ceremony and party in our backyard a few months later with another seventy or so friends from the States. The rabbi met me and welcomed me, no questions asked (hear that, Pope?). Jim's sister, Nancy, and his brothers, Arthur and Paul, held the chuppah. My maid of honor was Tammy, my longtime girlfriend and fellow journalist whose assignments in California, New York, and Miami had coincided with mine over the years. Jim's best man was his dad. My friends Elaine and Michele flew in from the East Coast. I hired a paella maker from San Diego, who set up his huge shallow pan on a gas grill in one corner of the backyard and was harassed for most of the early evening by salivating guests who wanted to know when it would be ready.

"It's ready now. Do you want me to serve?" the chef asked me several times. Rican that I was, I was convinced the guests would split after they ate. "No," I said.

Jim and I got the dancing going and partied like relaxed guests at our wedding all night. Arielle and Henry made cameo appearances. They had many friends among the wedding guests this time around, and they mostly held court in the rooms upstairs. Everything went according to plan, except I couldn't help but notice that my wedding dress felt like a corset, just a few months after the first wedding. The dress fit snugly in Puerto Rico, but in L.A. I was afraid the zipper would pop open. No, I was not pregnant. I was just heavier. I automatically gained ten pounds shortly after moving to Los Angeles because of all the driving. And I developed a sweet tooth eating like the third kid in the house—tacos, pasta, Nestlé Crunch Drumstick cones of vanilla ice cream dipped in chocolate with nuts. There was always ice cream in the freezer and cookies in the pantry.

This was one thing about stepmothering: You don't get pregnant, but you still get fat.

The weight might have also had something to do with another little habit that had crept up into my lifestyle—daily wine drinking. In New York I usually drank only when out with friends. As an attached and now married woman, I was putting away at least half a bottle of wine every night preparing dinner and eating with my hubby. It was so easy to do in California, where you could find great wines from Santa Ynez and Napa and Sonoma for under fifteen dollars at the local Vons. But I wasn't going to lie. I looked forward to that glass of wine more and more as things didn't go my way on the home front.

Our wonderful weddings behind us now, the goings-on in our household were still an issue. I felt the kids, not us adults, controlled the tone of our home. We were at the mercy of hormones. I had no power without Jim's support. I was always on guard for the next eruption that might ruin a dinner, a movie night, a birthday party, a vacation.

Oooooooommmmmmmmmmmmmmmmmmm.

Wasn't a married couple supposed to make decisions together, act like the co-chairs of a board? As the months passed, Jim and I fought in whispers. The most harmless conversation about the kids could devolve into a hideous fight. Even when we made up, I increasingly found myself at a low simmer. I felt Jim sometimes acted as if he needed to protect the kids from me. One night, he asked me to help Henry with his Spanish homework. As Henry and I sat down at the dining table I noticed Jim was making himself comfortable a few feet away at the kitchen table with a book. I shooed him away and later asked him what the hell did he think he was doing. At first he denied he had purposely stayed—"I just wanted to read"—but eventually the truth came out.

"It was the first time you helped him and I just wanted to make sure everything went smoothly."

For Henry or for me? And what exactly was he concerned about?

The next day, while we went about the house not speaking to each other, I heard Jim call out from the kitchen: "Want some breakfast?"

I was on the other side of the wall, reading in the living room, and welcomed the olive branch. I was about to answer him when I heard baby talk.

"Are you smiling? Why are you smiling? Life is good."

Got me!

When Jim was mad at me, he couldn't talk to his dog enough.

Meanwhile, the kids were growing into teenhood fast. They were gaining independence, with playdates turning into outings to the movies and to parties. Our active lives gave us all more breathing room, but I felt I was failing to forge a real relationship with them. I felt a hundred years old, not cool at all. When Jim's birthday rolled around, I saw the opportunity for a fun family time. I cooked a meal and lined up Arielle and Henry to help with chores. They did, gladly, and they were excited about the special occasion and cake. We had a nice dinner, and Jim and I lingered at the table after the kids went back upstairs to the computer and to watch TV. Henry had agreed to take care of the dishes, but when I called him down, he asked, "Why do I have to do this?" He was half kidding, half whining, and I just said: "Come on, it's your dad's birthday." It should have ended there, but Jim saw the exchange as a potential fight that he needed to avoid. He offered to help do the dishes. "No. It's your birthday!" I protested. "Henry can handle it." But the two were already working in tandem, Henry washing and Jim drying. I let them be. It was an innocuous disagreement. From a distance, the outcome might have even appeared to be endearing. But I felt pushed out again. I could insist on doing what I thought was right, regardless of whose feelings I trampled, and hope for change, or I could focus on my marriage and let Jim continue to be the single dad however he chose to do it. I had gone back and forth on this, until this birthday night when I decided to retreat for good.

"They" were not joking when they said marriage was work. On our first wedding anniversary, I got an expensive card and wrote a heartfelt message with words like "challenge" and "future." My always optimistic hubby made his own card and drew little hearts marching from the canyons of California to the sunrise of Puerto Rico and the words: "They just go on and on."

But I couldn't shake my frustrations at home. I felt unmoored. One day, I started to detach. I stayed late at work one night, or went out with friends another night. I did this on some of the nights the kids were home. Jim didn't like that I was skipping some family dinners. But the occasional respite helped me defer to Jim. It was either that or become the wicked stepmother. I wasn't thrilled with my choices.

Eddie, however, was all mine to mold. If he wasn't going to be my pet, he could at least be my pet project. I was not going to spend my hard-earned money on trainers for uncertain results, but I could try to teach this mutt obedience, some tricks even, and train him myself. It was a tall order. He didn't even come to me when summoned. It took at least three "Eddies" to get any reaction. The first "Eddie!" made him blink. The second "Eddie!" possibly prompted him to get up and find something to sniff at in the vicinity. The third "Eddie!" finally set him in my direction. "Eddie! Eddie! Eddie!"

This was the raw material I had to work with. But I was inspired by a story I wrote for the *Times* about the competitive world of canine freestyle dancing. Dogs can be trained not so much to dance as to weave, back up, turn around, and go through their owner's legs to the beat of music.

"It's more like modern dance than ballroom dancing," one dancing-dog owner explained. "It's interpretative dance to music."

I wasn't that impressed when I finally saw some of the dancing dogs in action. They went in and out of their owner's legs, they jumped on hind legs, but it was not dancing. It was boring until one owner told me freestyle had helped tame her misbehaving dog.

"They learn to focus on their owners rather than to have their own agenda," she said.

Eddie certainly had an agenda. But he did not even fetch, so dancing would have been like Princeton to a tot.

But if dogs could dance, our Eddie could surely heel, shake, and roll over. He was already so good at sitting.

"Shake!" I commanded one Saturday when he and I were home alone.

I grabbed his left front paw and showed him. Then I fed him a biscuit. "Good boy." He learned that trick pretty fast once he realized treats awaited. The results were so encouraging, so easy, that we soon moved on to rolling over.

"Sit!"

"Good boy."

"Down! Get down!"

This one seemed a little tougher. Eddie became confused and gave me his paw to shake.

"No. Down!" I pushed his body down and he finally let go.

"Roll over!"

I had to do that for him too as he went limp. What did this dog weigh? Forty-five pounds? Heavy. It was like trying to shove a dresser.

It took a few days of repetitive work, but he finally got it, sort of. Now when I commanded "Sit!" he flopped down and rolled over in one quick motion to get his biscuit sooner.

When I thought he was more or less ready, I promised Jim and the kids a surprise one evening after dinner. They gathered around and Eddie performed flawlessly to much wowing and laughter.

I was proud of him and proud of myself.

"See?" I told Jim telepathically. "It didn't kill the dog to experience some discipline."

I ambitiously turned from the power of the biscuit to Cesar Millan, whose show I discovered accidentally while flipping TV channels. *Dog Whisperer* was a hoot and I loved Millan's no-nonsense approach. You're the boss, the leader of the pack, and the dog must follow, not the other way around.

"If you don't become your dog's pack leader, he will assume that role and try to dominate you," he warned in his book *Cesar's Way*.

The antidote for a dog with issues, he advised, was exercise, discipline, and affection, "in that order!"

Sí!

I could do at least two of three. After all the touchy-feely advice from stepfamily expert books, I welcomed Millan's straightforward orders.

During our walks, Eddie usually strained at the leash as if he just got past airport security and his plane was about to leave. He wanted to smell the leaves, or charge another dog, or chase a squirrel. I now started to tug back to get him to heel and not walk in front of me anymore.

"Heel, Eddie!"

He seemed surprised at the change in our routine and kept pulling, throwing his weight to one side and making choking sounds. So annoying. But I persisted with Millan's way, trying to give off "calm-assertive" energy that just cried out "leader."

When that didn't work, I yelled.

"From now on, you heel! Heel! Heel!"

Eddie did not like it but he had no choice. I tugged hard whenever he yanked forward.

I next tried to yank Jim's collar. We needed to present a united front with Eddie too. But Jim just laughed when I explained the training and asked him to reinforce it when he took Eddie out.

"Good luck," he said.

I was not amused. "I'm serious, Jim."

"He's like most dogs," he said, "so excited when you put him on a leash, he's constantly pulling you. It's what most young dogs do."

"So you don't want to even try it."

"No. This is going to be a futile and time-consuming effort and accomplish nothing."

"So you won't want to work with me?"

"This is not about you, darling. I'm just trying to do the sensible thing. I've never cared to put that much time and attention to the dog. I'm not into all this training stuff. I just kind of let him be a dog. That's good enough for me."

"But this goes hand in hand with other types of behavior. He still sits on sofas, he still tries to sneak into our bedroom. This is supposed to nurture the idea that there are things he cannot do."

"I just want him to be a happy guy and a good companion."

Jim just didn't want to upset Eddie. Every so often I'd go through our tricks so Eddie wouldn't forget them, hiding the biscuit behind my back until he performed the shake–roll-over bit more or less perfectly. My husband acted as if I were lashing his dog like a lion tamer. "He's waiting for the biscuit, darling," he said with a sour smile as he watched me one morning rehearsing Eddie a few times without rewarding him.

I prodded Eddie to roll over on the hardwood floor of the kitchen, but he balked. He just refused. I didn't know why I even bothered. My teaching Eddie tricks had not brought us any closer. He still pestered me. He still did whatever he felt like.

"He won't roll over on the hardwood floor," Jim urged me. "Do it on the carpet."

"Who's the trainer?" I said, giving up.

I had more important concerns. We had a dinner party coming up on Saturday and we needed to figure out what to do about the dog. California's energy czar was among a group of ten friends we had invited for a grilled salmon dinner. We had met the state energy official at another friend's a few weeks before and it had not gone that well. That friend, Tom, held salon-type lunches on Saturdays and I found myself sitting next to the energy czar as a joint made its way to me. I had a decision to make—pass it on to the state official or send it on its journey back to the potheads who thought it was a good idea to light up. I chose the latter, but both czar and I were silently mortified.

The night of our dinner party there was no pot, only Eddie to worry about. We usually crated him during parties and Eddie was fine with it, but a friend would sooner or later ask "Where's Eddie?" and then spring him free. I didn't like it because it reminded me of what a former ambassador to Belize once told me she did at her parties—she would set her dogs loose to let guests know it was time to go home. Not exactly diplomatic. I didn't want anyone at my parties to get the idea we were throwing them out. But Eddie always had a Che Guevara in our crowd eager to liberate him.

"Let's crate him before the guests show up," I told Jim. "Not everyone is a dog lover, and the energy czar mentioned to you that he's afraid of dogs, remember? I don't want Eddie under the table vacuuming crumbs and trying to lick hands during dinner anyway."

"Sure, of course."

The night of the party, as we set out hors d'oeuvres in the backyard and showtime approached, I told Jim, "Let's crate Eddie now."

"We can do it when we sit down to dinner," Jim said. "We'll be in the backyard for cocktails and he'll just be busy running around."

"I don't think that's a good idea if the guy is afraid of dogs."

"It'll be fine."

The czar was Jim's guest, not mine, so I backed off.

Our guests arrived and we gathered outside with cocktails in hand. The state official sat at our oval-shaped glass table on the patio with a few other friends. I was in the kitchen preparing trays in between sips of a martini when I looked over and saw Eddie jump on the czar, trying to get to a morsel of Manchego cheese.

"Eddie! Jim!" I screamed, spilling half of my drink on the floor.

Jim ran over to the table still holding his glass of scotch and peeled his beast off the petrified man. *That's* when he crated Eddie.

I was beyond upset. This was also the day I first noticed floaters in my eyes.

It may have been all an overreaction (on the energy czar's part too), but I had had it with Jim's leniency. The Latina in me couldn't bear the thought of making a guest uncomfortable. The sense of hospitality captured in the phrase *"Mi casa es su casa"* was ingrained. The energy czar never recovered. Even after Eddie was safely crated away, the poor guy ate looking over his shoulder.

That night, I conflated kids and dog and troubled marriage and felt furious at my husband. It was obvious that Jim, whether consciously or subconsciously, was not ready for a co—head of household, or, yes, let's go there, even marriage. He may have adored me, but he had me pegged. I felt he encouraged my efforts to put my stamp on the blended family and then sabotaged me. Now I was upset even at parties.

There was really no point in any further delay.

We—I—needed help.

Eight

Stepparenting 101: The Fun House

Right now I'm locked away in my room, bawling my eyes out . . . again. Part of me knows I shouldn't be this upset. There's no one who understands, who can help talk me down, so I spiral through rage and grief."

Thank God that was not me. This particular horror story was from a member of my Yahoo! support group. My own troubles seemed trivial next to the stepmom in the middle of her husband's nasty custody battle, or the one with the drug-addicted stepson, or the one raising four stepkids who didn't get a Mother's Day card, or the one whose husband ignored her when his kids were around. Boy, could these stepmoms vent. I took solace in that at least I wasn't going through *that*. But I could relate. In fact, I was a cliché. A few hours online and it was obvious many stepmoms shared uncannily similar experiences. Feeling isolated. Check. Doubting yourself. Check. Feeling resentful, jealous, inadequate—check, check, check. We all felt like we woke up one day in the wrong reality show. No matter how much in love we were, it wasn't just about the love relationship.

Already years since the wedding, the family blending was still a problem. My constant reminder was the dog resting flat on the floor right now, following my movements in the kitchen like a crocodile tracking his prey. His thoughts came through clearly.

"She eats with my guy, she sleeps with my guy, she gets my guy's attention. I'll harass her until she hightails it out of here."

Suck it up, dog.

What did I think my life as a stepmom would be like? In my fantasy, I envisioned us gathering at the end of the day, all of us asking, "How was your day?" The kids would tell me they didn't like their teachers, and I would tell them about the nun who spanked me in first grade for talking in the line for the bathroom, making them realize they didn't have it so bad. I envisioned myself as their confidante, the one they'd come to when they were angry with their parents. I'd be funny and silly, they'd laugh at my jokes. I'd be a mentor, a role model, a positive influence, the voice of reason in their emotionally charged lives, a friend. I envisioned hugging my way through the rough patches. I envisioned having a family (with no dog but perhaps a rabbit).

Back to earth, I realized I had been overexposed to Hollywood endings. The advice from real-life stepmoms was brutal.

"Get your armor on," one Yahoo! stepmom wrote. "It's a painful road."

"Behave like a potted plant," another one said. In other words: Zip it up.

"Have a time-out room for yourself, complete with a lock."

"Get out."

That last bit was the reaction to a stepmom who wrote that she had left her life in California to move to Florida for marriage. The BM, or biological mom in stepmom jargon, was "a control freak" who for the past two years had tried to alienate her eight-year-old daughter from the father. The stepmom felt she was "a dumping ground for both the mom and the daughter's anger about this divorce." The stepmom now struggled with feelings of depression. "I feel like I am in the twilight zone," she wrote.

But after all that, she was staying put.

"I gained an amazing man," she explained.

You could feel the collective head nods through the computer. That was the irony. When our husbands showed their commitment to their families, their big hearts, it made us love these amazing men more, even if the maddening family goings-on took us straight to vodka martinis (shaken, please).

The consensus, I learned a bit late, was that it was best to enter a stepchild's life before the age of ten or after the age of fifteen, to avoid the terrifying terrain known as puberty. I had perversely come in past the Chuck E. Cheese's birthday party stage and just in time for the door-slamming phase. So much for my investigative reporting skills. With the kids already in high school, I was still a pinball in the household—one still hoping to land in just the right place.

I had tried books and the patience of friends seeking advice. After the mishap involving one energy czar, I'd also turned to online support groups. I voraciously read my Yahoo! e-mails late at night for nuggets of wisdom. Much of the information from my stepmom sisterhood alarmed me, but there was a lot that gave me comfort and hope too. Many stepmoms wrote to say "Hang in there!" or "It's all worth it." There were happy endings. Some were generous with ideas for coping in the meantime.

"Find a way to exercise at least three times a week."
"Take time for yourself—take night classes, craft classes, book groups, or just sit in a bookstore coffee shop and read."
"Don't forgo happy hours after work and shopping and weekend trips with your girlfriends."

I revved up my social calendar and became a health nut. I drove forty-five minutes in traffic to a Zumba class. I started my mornings twice a week with Pilates. I found a place with forty-dollar-an-hour massages. I breathed and om'ed for dear life. When a literary agent spotted a Sunday Styles story I wrote on environmentally sensitive weddings, she encouraged me to write a book and I eagerly took on what eventually became *Green Wedding: Planning Your Eco-friendly Celebration*. Jim, an author himself (he wrote *Burning Down the House*, a book about the fall of E. F Hutton), cheered me on. Book writing took over more and more of my weekends and free time. On weekdays, I immersed myself deeper into my work at the *Times*.

The distractions and work helped, but my beloved husband and I still needed to achieve a workable home life. Suffice it to say that after several years of marriage, I was still not one of the peeps. I hadn't gotten much beyond the hi-and-bye stage with the kids as they came and went in the endless shuttling between their mom and pop worlds. I helped the kids pick presents for their father. I cooked chicken wings, enchiladas, and other fun dishes for them (even prompting a friend of Henry's to tell him midway through ecstatic gorging: "You're so lucky!"). I went to movies and shared dinners with them. But I barely scratched the surface of involvement. There were many lines I felt I couldn't cross in order to avoid ripples of conflict. Sometimes I felt like I lived with strangers.

I loved my husband more than ever as I lived a double life—half the week, when Jim and I were alone, we were each the person the other met. The other half, I was sidelined in my own home. I found Jim uncompromising when it came to his children. I looked for more ways to disengage and make myself scarce.

But there was only so much escaping I could do. Jim and I agreed we needed to see a therapist. For me, to go to a shrink required outgrowing some cultural apprehensions. The conventional wisdom when I was growing up was that only crazy people needed one. I had never felt the need to pay someone to listen to my problems, even in therapy-happy New York. I had plenty of girlfriends for that. But at some point I realized what an imposition that was, how boring I sounded, and I started holding back. A professional would offer a safe, neutral space to let it rip. I was overcoming my misgivings. There was no way around the need for someone to help us bridge our differences. All the experts seemed to agree that the job of blending a family was often too big for just two people. Making the emotional mechanics of two grown-ups jibe in these tense situations required distance and knowledge. Some experts didn't even like the word "blend," calling the term misleading. People were not ingredients that could be poured together in this vessel known as marriage and blended into a mix, they warned. Children, particularly, kept their old connections and loyalties. They'd always have two families, not just the one, no matter how much blending may be attempted.

And need I say Eddie was just another difficult personality in the household, another riptide trying to crash my marriage onto the rocks? I exaggerate, but he certainly was not helping. He added to the tensions, the bad energy. Sometimes I came home from work and found husband, kids, and dog all snuggled up watching a movie on the couch. The dog looked the smuggest of them all, at least until a doorbell rang on TV and he whizzed past me like a bullet to greet no one at our front door.

Nitwit.

I was aware that Eddie brought out the worst in me, and I tried to be the adult *Homo sapiens*. But on bad days, I begrudged him his simple, coddled life—not a care in the world, lots of scratching behind the ears, free food, sweet nothings, and fresh air. Few things gave me more pleasure at times than to sit on Jim's lap and smooch with him—while I watched Spots go berserk. Sometimes, if Eddie was in the backyard sunning himself, I purposely made a racket as I stomped up the steps to Jim's office. Within seconds I'd hear Eddie scrambling to get up, get inside, and catch up to me so he could beat me to the prize, whimpering all the way from sunny backyard to den. If I timed it right, he reached me just as I shut the door in his spotted face. I was trying to induce a canine heart attack, if there was such a thing.

I no longer left the kitchen glass door open while Eddie went out to doze in the backyard. Why should I have risked Manson-like murder for the dog? The garden-gate latch was broken and it could be pushed open easily. There was always a chance he "accidentally" could escape. Wouldn't that be just awful? So what? Not my dog. Really, if he disappeared, I wouldn't miss him. I wouldn't miss the jealousy, the competitiveness, the cold shoulder. Nope.

My dream almost came true one afternoon. Jim and the kids were out and I was at the computer in my office. Eddie was in the backyard, unattended, lounging on the grass, squinting at the sun, trying to decide if he should roll in the grass or just snooze some more. When he felt like it, he scratched the glass door of the kitchen, signaling he was done with his sunbathing. But the doorwoman happened to be busy, deeply involved in reading something for work. I ignored him. He scratched a bit more. Still reading. Patience was not Eddie's forte, but eventually he stopped. In the silence that followed, he pushed through the busted gate and escaped into the driveway. Then, instead of turning right out of the back alley to go visit with his coyote friends, he made a left, which brought him around to the front of the house. Within minutes, I heard scratching again, this time at the front door. Impressive, I had to admit. When it came to self-interest, the wily mutt was nothing but brilliant.

One sleepless night I finally dozed off and had a dream. I was hosting some sort of party and I was grilling ribs. I ran out of meat, so I decided to roast Eddie *a la varita*, like a Puerto Rican–style suckling pig. The dream was really a nightmare because I could see Eddie becoming hairless, looking at me as he acquired the reddish-brown hue of well-done pork. I realized what I had done and dreaded facing Jim. My sister was at the party and she knew what had happened. In a matter of seconds Jim would learn the ghastly truth. I woke up.

I wasn't proud of myself.

I knew I walked a fine line with Eddie. Jim adored his buddy. If Eddie barked at an imaginary fly, going batty for a moment, my reaction was to yell, "Eddie! Shut up!" But not Jim. His relationship with Eddie was a search for meaning, understanding, insights. It was as if he were the dog.

"Thank you for protecting us, you big galoot," he said. "I know, I know, I know. Grrrrr. Grrrrrrrrrr."

Both the kids and I were victims of this attention hog. As soon as we sat down to eat in the backyard or indoors, Eddie would start rolling on the grass or the carpet, squirming and scratching his back, snorting and sneezing, hamming it up until all conversation stopped and we had no choice but to watch him.

Also typical in the Sterngold sitcom:

"Dad! Have you seen Dad, Mia?"

"He's walking Eddie."

"Jim! Have you seen your father, Henry?"

"He's walking Eddie."

The two were inseparable. If Eddie made it to the car for an outing, he whimpered from the back of the station wagon all the way to our destination and back.

"He's the only dog I know who doesn't like a car ride," Jim said in wonder.

But that wasn't it. Eddie just didn't like that he wasn't riding on his boyfriend's lap. When we could finally shake the dog to go out, dog drama unfolded. Eddie let his anxiety over our impending departure be loudly known at the first hint of preparation. The mere sound of the shower or a change of clothes could set off whimpering. He'd stand frozen, head down, eyes doleful, anxiously waiting for Jim by the bathroom door. He looked so pathetic you'd think his master had been lost at sea.

Eddie remained concerned but calm as the kids and I filed out the garage door. But he started with his little yelps of misery once Jim grabbed his sunglasses and keys.

"It's okay, buddy, we're going to be back soon," Jim said, scratching and eliciting even louder whimpers. "I'll give you a biscuit. I'll come back and scratch you soon."

In the car, meanwhile, the rest of us waited.

But I couldn't help loving Jim for loving Eddie. He was a serious guy, a serious journalist, talking endlessly about nuclear weapons policy or criminal justice reform, and then, there he was, smitten with this strange creature.

A creature-thing that startled me when he sidled up to me one morning while I sat on the plush carpet in my office, paying bills.

"Eddie! What do you want?"

He had breached the off-limits area and he looked scared. I heard Jim whistling and realized he was chasing the dog around the house to give him a bath. Eddie hated water. In his desperate effort to hide from Jim, he tried to cozy up on my lap, his front paws on my chest as he wriggled his butt into position. His whimpers only got louder as Jim approached.

"Right here!" Jim commanded, trying to get him out to the driveway, where canine baths were dispensed. "Hey, get over here!"

The whimpers reached operatic notes as I pushed Eddie away. "Forget it, buddy." He then resorted to his most loathsome trick: rolling on his back to spread his legs and let out a little arc of pee. On my carpet.

"Get him out of here, please!" I begged Jim.

My husband picked him up and carried him out like a squirming sack of potatoes. "You big galoot."

I got to the kitchen to get a towel and some cleaner, but when I heard Jim turn on the water, I raced outside so I wouldn't miss one of my favorite shows: "Five Minutes of Misery in Eddie's Charmed Life." The comedy was always the same, but I never tired of it.

"Is that so bad?" Jim asked as his dog stood in the driveway, getting soaped up with a sad and defeated face.

Eddie looked genuinely anguished, but I felt not a bit of compassion.

"I don't think so. See? It's a hot day. I'm going to soak you up. No! Don't you dare shake! No shaking! We're going to get nice and clean."

Jim scrubbed so vigorously he was almost out of breath.

"A little scratch there. A little scratch before that ear. You're going to smell sweet for a change, right? Whoa! No shaking! Okay, getting close. Homestretch. There you go, there you go. Right? See? Don't look so unhappy."

Eddie attempted to bolt, but Jim grabbed him in time. "Don't even think of getting on the grass. Now you shake. Now comes the good part. This is the part you like. A full-body scratch with the towel."

Over, and under, and around. Then the final step: brushing. The bath was done in less than ten minutes.

"Good doggie, Eddie. You're such a good boy."

I smiled as the job was finished and Eddie didn't look any more appealing. But Jim looked adorable. He was such a good daddy.

And such a rock in the middle of turmoil. In the thick of the recession of the late 2000s, the *San Francisco Chronicle* was going through a big financial squeeze, with layoffs and buyouts, and they had eliminated Jim's position. My husband was forced to take a buy-out and look for another job, again. He turned to magazines and lined up freelancing assignments for *Mother Jones* and others to write about the California prison system and President George W. Bush's efforts to restart the nation's long-neglected nuclear weapons complex. He also spent several months as a researcher and writer at the Center for Investigative Reporting, working on a project on the prospects for coal production and clean coal technology.

He knew he had me to lean on, both emotionally and financially, if it came to that. He knew I loved him and would support his career choices.

Still, we needed a professional, at hourly rates of two hundred to three hundred dollars, to intervene. We found our first shrink specializing on stepfamilies through a friend of Jim's. I was nervous at first but soon relaxed sitting on the couch with Jim by my side. A good forty minutes of the hourly session were spent going over our backgrounds. Then we dug in, speaking of our conflict in neutral tones, sounding like the articulate, reasonable people we had each married. But after a few sessions, Therapist #1 concluded that our problem was communication. Excuse me? I thought our problem was that we disagreed on parenting issues and couldn't find common ground. Jim felt it was something in between. He believed there were communication issues, that we were talking past each other.

The therapist gave us exercises. "When you tell her something, ask her to repeat what you just said to make sure she listened, and vice versa."

Okeydokey. It sounded so reasonable. In the middle of an argument, though, the exercise came off as patronizing and made us angrier.

"Are you listening to me?" I asked during a fight. "Repeat what I just said."

"I'm not going to repeat what you just said."

"Repeat it!"

After several sessions of discussing communication skills, Jim and I had both had it with Therapist #1. We had fallen into a pattern. We nodded in agreement and left his office feeling hopeful. The session was terrific, we both felt the therapist had guided us to a better place. But by the time we reached the parking lot, it was obvious we each had just heard the part about what the other person had to change. Another three hundred dollars wasted.

I got the name of another therapist from another stepmom I met by chance. She suggested going at it solo. "He will tell you how to protect yourself," she told me, jotting down the guy's name and number. "He saved my life."

Therapist #2 was older, a more fatherly figure. I went and he listened. I told him Jim was a wonderful husband and father. I told him sometimes I berated myself for not letting it go at that. Here I was being a nag when he was pursuing the noble goals of fatherhood. But I couldn't help feeling the way I was feeling. The bottom line for me was that my husband didn't trust me as co-chair of the family board and that I didn't feel comfortable in my own home. My husband's children were not mine to even hug and kiss without it feeling like I was overstepping or that there would be repercussions. With the kids, too much affection could trigger parental loyalty issues; too much control could trigger rebellion against the father's wife trying to take over. With Jim, too much assertiveness just triggered another fight. I told him this was the thing about stepmothering: when all was said and done, the kids still weren't yours.

But in the end, I told Therapist #2, our different approaches to raising a family were not as much the issue as Jim's belief that he could juggle the roles of father and husband separately, as though there were two Jims. It felt to me as if he had tried to build a wall between these two people, hoping perhaps that the rest of us wouldn't notice, or wouldn't mind. I understood that Jim was under an array of crushing pressures as a divorced father. I so wanted to help him. But, even so, I was given no responsibility and reaped no reward.

I didn't stop talking for almost the whole hour. Therapist #2 nodded empathetically and seemed to agree with me on everything. Then he talked, and I listened.

Session 1: The takeaway: "Stay in the hurt." Hurt is better than anger.

Session 2: When having a talk, ask Jim to repeat what I just said to make sure he heard me. (Ugh).

Session 3: Make "I" statements only. "I" feel like an outsider, not a real partner. "I" feel that you humor me when you say you share my goals and will try to do better next time.

Session 4: When making amends, say I'm sorry and shut up. Do not follow with "if" or "but."

Session 5: Ask "what" and "how" questions, not "why." "What happened?" "How can I help you?"

Session 6: Forgive.

Session 7: Be gentle and warm. Try to get along, not to be right.

Do you want to be right or do you want to be happy, the shrink asked. Happy, I wanted to scream.

"Define your role," the shrink said. "What do you want to be—a stepmother or just Mia? In the meantime, be yourself. Show them a different way. Give them love, the real power you have. No one can fight against that."

Did I have it in me? Why was I so unyielding on issues of authority and respect? The bottom line was that Arielle and Henry were both good kids. But it was such a visceral reaction. Jim suspected there was something else eating at me. He was afraid I might be feeling cheated out of having my own children. When we met, we discussed adopting our own child but never followed through. We were young enough to consider having our own children, but we had so much on our plate in those first few years. Relocation, change of jobs for both of us, remarriage, new-family dynamics. I reassured him that was not it, and it really wasn't. It could have been an amazing experience for us, but neither one of us wanted it badly enough to pursue it and I was at peace with that. If anything cheated me out of having children it was coming of age in the 1970s, when the feminist message to ambitious young women was to plan a career, not motherhood.

So what was it? Didn't I love my husband enough to follow his lead? I was so confused. And scared. In a recurring nightmare, I'm single again after Jim and I have called it quits. I'm distraught. "How could I have fucked it up?" I ask myself in the dream. When I wake up, I have to wipe my face of cold tears.

I abandoned Therapist #2 and looked for someone to tell me point-blank that I was wrong. I found her through a website for blended families—Sheena, my very own stepmom life coach. For sixty dollars an hour, my coach would help me resolve conflicts, deal with the emotional baggage, and reach my goal of a harmonious home.

Our phone sessions felt like a breath of fresh air.

"It's important for you to remember that your level of concern does not match your ability to act," no-nonsense Sheena told me. "Jim is driving the bus and even though you're a front-seat passenger and can help determine the direction of the bus, ultimately Jim is the driver."

Rise above the day-to-day details and the minutiae, Sheena ordered me.

"Ignore the things that are none of your business, or can't be fixed or influenced by you anyway, and focus on the prize, which is your marriage."

Will do!

The next time I sat at the dinner table and one or the other kid, or their father, acted out in a manner that would have made my mother reach for her flyswatter, I tried to imagine I was the neighbor, just visiting for a meal, and this had nothing to do with me. I reminded myself that a stepmother is not the mother. I repeated, like a mantra, the advice of my many advisers: I was to be more like a consultant. Resist the urge to lecture or correct. Speak up only to reinforce the positive. Wear your poker face. But I couldn't. I felt like I was about to explode. It was so against my nature, my gut, to just sit there. This was my family too, and I wanted to see success. I wanted to grab everybody by the shoulders and shout: "Do it my way! You're all headed for the cliff!"

But not even Eddie was agreeable. In fact, in the middle of all the tension, Eddie just wore me down. Just now I forgot to close the door to my office and found him comfortably laid out on my Italian designer love seat. My first thought: What could I do to this filthy dog without getting arrested? I grabbed him by the collar and dragged him down and out of the office in one strong sweep.

Jim heard the commotion and came down to get his dog.

"He's completely untrustworthy," I said.

Eddie got on his hind legs to put two paws on my belly, as if to say "I'm sorry." Jim melted. I acknowledged the sudden act (show) of contrition and tap-tap-tapped Eddie's head, but I was skeptical. Even when I reached out to him now, seeing an opening, he stepped back, cringing at my touch, jerking back his head as if I had burned him with cigarettes or beat him with a stick all his life. When I grabbed his head, insisting on petting him, he stood still for three seconds before he pulled back little by little, as if he couldn't stand my touch.

"E-weirdo, why don't you love me?"

That night, he followed me to the kitchen as I fetched a glass of water before going to bed. In the dark and quiet kitchen his eyes glistened, like the dog in *Children of the Corn*, and I hurried back upstairs just in case he decided to finally attack.

Was I going batty? I never brought up the dog during therapy sessions—at three hundred dollars an hour, *that* would have been crazy. I still had friends for that. They listened for free.

"Jim just uses his junkyard dog to disappear when he doesn't want to talk," I complained to my friend Lynn over drinks at a tapas bar near the *Times* bureau. "In the middle of an argument he always gets this urge to walk Eddie and it's 'See you later.'"

Lynn, who lived in New York but traveled to L.A. often to see family, didn't like Eddie either. She was a cat person. After Jim and I met, she was among the girlfriends who told me I was obsessing too much about the dog.

"I worry that, here you've met a great guy, and the dog is going to fuck it up."

When Lynn and Eddie finally met after I moved to California, I asked for her assessment.

"I thought he'd be filthy dirty because of the way you described him. I expected him to have yellow drool and sharp teeth and red eyes and be farting all the time. But he's very clean."

Yet Lynn was still firmly in my corner.

"Of course you're upset," she now told me at the tapas bar as she speared a bacalao croquette with a toothpick. "They are running roughshod over you."

Thanks, honey.

One night as I lay in bed, I felt my chest tighten strangely. I tried to relax and fall asleep, but for the next few days I was conscious of this odd pressure in my chest. It felt like a strap was pulled tight across it and at times it even hurt a little. I told Jim and he acted calm, but he was a little alarmed and urged me to see a doctor. When I finally got myself checked out, it turned out that all was well. But whether the pain was real or imagined, I felt my body was sending me a message: I can't take it anymore. I was tired of walking on eggshells. I was tired of schedules that I knew little, if anything, about: vacation plans, decisions about whether Arielle was ready to learn to drive or whether Henry could have a drum set in the house. I was the consultant no one consulted. My efforts to try to disengage, to compartmentalize, weren't working—my chest was telling me that much. Maybe I should have cried more. Jim left me reassuring, loving notes on the kitchen table. He bought me flowers. My husband was my life, my support, my adviser, my lover, my love—I would never renounce him. But I reached the conclusion that we couldn't live together.

Perhaps blending a family was just an exceptional feat—doable for some but impossible for most. Perhaps the situation was so unnatural that there was no way to make it work without making somebody unhappy. Our situation was also a function of our inexperience and lack of preparation, but how can you prepare for stepparenting? Stepkids will ignore you, they will run hot and cold, and sooner or later someone will hurl the B-word at you, other stepmoms warned, and they were right. But everyone was going through their own struggles and a challenging family dynamic was to be expected. With some work, so was genuine affection, eventually. What came as a surprise to me was how my instincts seemed to fail me, how self-doubt took over and threw me off balance as I had to learn a whole other way of being. I admitted my shortcomings and I apologized for them. Perhaps there was another way. One morning, I found it on the pages of my own newspaper. There, in front of me as I drank my mud-thick coffee, was a story about the experiences of couples who lived in two households. The arrangement even had a name—L.A.T., for "living apart together." Experts cited in the story particularly recommended it for blended families with children who "are so vulnerable to internecine resentments and power struggles."

Oh my God. I read on.

"Although social pressures encourage stepfamilies blending," said Jeannette Lofas, a clinical social worker and founder of the Stepfamily Foundation, "only one out of three stepfamilies survive. I always say to people, Would you go on a plane to San Francisco with your child if you had a two-thirds chance of not surviving it?"

Once again, brutal. But to me, what resonated in the article was the success of couples who had tried L.A.T. lifestyles. They were unanimous that their marriages and long-term relationships were stronger, and had lasted, because they had room to be themselves.

The approach was so logical, so sensible. Jim could parent however he wanted without my interference. I could give him the support he needed without feeling robbed of my identity. The kids would be fine. They lived in their own busy worlds and they still had their mom and dad full-time. Any threat I may have posed to them—of stealing their father away, of competing for motherly love—would recede. I could still hold on to the picture of a happy stepfamily around the dinner table, someday. And if Jim and I split up, there wouldn't be any custody battles—he could have the dog!

"Look!" I told Jim, showing him the paper. Jim read the story with a pained look. He had his own disappointments too. He didn't get the marriage he signed up for either. He also felt sad, with a spouse who was too unbending. He felt I sat inside a fortress and didn't allow myself to be vulnerable. I agreed I had built up a wall that got higher and higher the less I was trusted. I didn't know how to gain that trust. He didn't understand why I was so unhappy. But we both wanted to save the marriage. He too wanted to bury his anger and preserve the support, inspiration, and respect, he told me. He too wanted to recapture the passion and "the spiritual high a true meeting of our souls can provide."

The idea of living apart was scary when we first discussed it. The experiment could go terribly wrong. But the risk seemed within acceptable levels and we began to warm up to the concept of separate homes as a viable option. As we tried to decide what to do, the *Times* called. They wanted me back in New York.

Nine

Somebody's Got to Go

The call came from the top editor in charge of breaking bad news. Because of layoffs in the newsroom, she told me, they wanted me back in New York along with another reporter in the *Times*'s L.A. bureau.

The *Times* was eliminating some hundred or so newsroom jobs. I was about one year short of maxing out on my national bureau rotation, usually about five years, so of course I feared the worst. They knew I was married with young stepkids and couldn't just pick up and leave. Didn't they remember this was exactly what forced Jim to quit? The paper was now offering buyouts. Should I take the money and run?

I didn't want the editor on the line to mince words. "Do you guys want me to quit? I need to know."

"No, we want you to stay," she reassured me.

I was in the backyard, where I had been reading clips for a story, and Jim was upstairs in the den, working.

"Jiiimmm!" I screamed at his office window as I hung up.

He came down and I told him the news.

"It's not a complete surprise," he said soothingly. "Let's talk through the options. Pull up stakes and go, or stay. There's freelancing. You can look at things involving Hispanic issues. It doesn't have to be in journalism."

We tackled professional concerns first because it was easier than talking about us. But I didn't appreciate that he started off the discussion by suggesting I could leave my job. I wasn't done with my career yet. But I also knew I was past the stage of the professional taking precedence over the personal. I knew I'd do whatever was best for our marriage.

That night, as I tried to fall asleep, I thought, Wait a minute . . . We had just been handed a gift! This was the temporary separation we so desperately needed, without the guilt. After toying with the idea of maintaining two households, we now faced a whole different set of options. The kids were not little anymore. Arielle and Henry were progressing through high school. The marriage needed a breather. Wouldn't a move to New York allow Jim and I to stay together even if apart? We were experts at long-distance love. It seemed counterintuitive, but it was a solution. I could keep the job and the marriage. Funny how the *Times* facilitated the marriage by transferring me to L.A. and now it was coming to rescue us by taking me—and eventually Jim—back to New York.

I was dizzy with a mix of emotions. I was excited. Jim was not. He was facing the relocation (or dislocation, as he saw it) of his wife. It would be an anxious, trying time for him with my leaving. He was of two minds—he wasn't up for another JetBlue relationship, but he understood that in these tough times in our industry, we were fortunate that I still had my job, and that wasn't a small thing.

Ultimately, Jim came through and supported my decision to move to New York, like I knew he would. We were always in agreement when it was about just us. Even if it took years, we knew we'd always be together. I was certain everyone was headed for their own exciting futures. In no time the kids would be applying to colleges. Our relationships would all move to the next stage. We'd get a chance to redefine our bonds. We may have survived after all. Only one thing would make everything perfect.

"We'd have to find a new home for Eddie," I told Jim in the glow of our newfound understanding. "He won't survive the city."

I was getting ahead of myself, but I was anticipating that Eddie would become an even bigger issue down the line if Jim insisted on taking him to New York. I truly believed that a dog whose life revolved around roaming in more than three thousand square feet of house, sunbathing in the backyard, rolling in the grass, and terrorizing other dogs in the neighborhood (except the two badass Pomeranians) could not possibly be happy around concrete in nasty weather. But, mostly, I saw my chance to get rid of Eddie. I needed to plant the idea.

The thought of the brute in my small one-bedroom in New York was horrific. Even for Jim and me, the eight-hundred-square-foot space would be tight given the downgrade from our gigantic house. Eddie would go berserk in such tight quarters. His barking would prompt complaints from the neighbors. His spiky hair would flutter around with even less room to land; it would collect into even bigger fur balls. He wouldn't be able to sunbathe or roll in the grass to scratch his back anymore. My co-op didn't even allow dogs in its grass areas. He'd become depressed—another neurotic New Yorker—and bite the doorman. We'd get sued, maybe kicked out by the co-op board, and be forced to move to New Jersey.

Eddie and I didn't get along and New York was stressful enough. We'd have plenty of time for me to find him a nice home.

"He's my dog" was all Jim said.

But he looked pensive, as if he could entertain the notion of life without Eddie, leaving the door open for me to hope . . . but not for too long, I knew. Have I mentioned Jim's a Libra? That's the sign of people who pretend to weigh every alternative endlessly only to end up doing exactly what they wanted all along.

I left my husband to his transparent thoughts to go back to worrying about finding a job within my job. I was told I was going back to Metro and needed to talk to the Metro editor about my next assignment. For me, Metro had been home. It was where I began at the *Times* when I was hired from the *Examiner* and where I had wanted to return after my five-year stint in Florida and the Caribbean. I welcomed the chance to reinvent myself once again, especially by going back to hard news, to writing about more sober issues than dancing dogs and Hollywood celebrities.

In New York, one of the Metro writers who took a buyout, Anthony, covered the environment. I wrote a proposal for the environmental beat easily, using much of what I learned writing *Green Wedding*, which was about to be released early the next year. I got the beat and was expected to start the new job after the summer, in three months. Three months to say good-bye to my family and to L.A. Whatever New Yorkers thought they knew about California, it was usually reduced to mockery. The plastic surgery faces. The tiers of exclusivity. Even going-away parties like the one for our colleague (who is married to a movie studio chief) had an A-list and a B-list. But it took living in L.A. to realize that there was a real upside to all that sprawl, bad air, and gridlock on the freeway. L.A. didn't get the civic boosterism New York enjoyed, but it was a real city, with enough culture, diversity, and fine dining to keep any New Yorker busy for a lifetime (I found even better pizza). But the biggest appeal was the lifestyle that came with good weather. Fine weather doesn't mean just sunny days. It means a different life altogether. It gets you out of the house and into the outdoors—to walk, to hike, to become intimate with your surroundings, to warm your soul and make you aware of life's pleasures, even little ones, such as eating in the backyard under starry skies.

We lived close enough to the Pacific that it cleared the smog and we could see stars. I was already missing our backyard. And I wouldn't miss the driving, but I'd miss my company Chevy. How could I live again without a trunk? It was my big purse. The impending separation was making me nostalgic even before I left. I began to suffer mini bouts of panic.

At yoga church the next Sunday, I tried hard to relax.

"Feel your stress dissolve," the instructor said.

My anxiety felt hard as a boulder. I lay on my mat, trying to fend off the assault of worrywart clouds that instead of floating away ganged up to attack me. One of them was in the shape of a huge black hole swallowing all our money. We were going to have to sell our house at a loss in a down market. Most of my savings were tied up in that house. Jim's too. But he wouldn't be able to afford the house by himself once I retrieved my New York apartment from the tenants and resumed paying its mortgage. Jim would have to get a rental in the Palisades. We were forced to put the house on the market now to leave ample time for a sale.

To prepare our house for viewing, we repainted the walls and refinished the wood floors on the first floor. That meant no paws allowed to scratch the three-thousand-dollar job. I bought Eddie two pairs of booties online, but he couldn't stand them. His legs buckled when he tried to walk in them. He looked like a newborn horse learning to stand and take the first tentative steps, with legs spread out at funny angles. He bit the booties off. Good-bye, thirty-five dollars. We had to keep him upstairs, positioning his crate in front of the stairway to block access. He whimpered at first, confused at the inexplicable curtailment of his freedoms. But he still had the second floor to romp around on and eventually seemed to accept his fate.

"At least he's not trying to kill himself anymore by jumping over the crate," I told Jim.

We were both leaning against the wall in the hallway at the top of the stairs, arms crossed, as we assessed our dog. How much of our limited time on this earth did we spend talking about Eddie? Too much.

"Are you trying to kill yourself?" Jim asked Eddie.

The dog tilted his head as if communicating that he indeed had considered suicide, until a dust ball distracted him. Maybe he could live in an apartment after all. I brushed aside the thought.

We made a list of the furniture I'd take. When Jim and I had moved in together, both sets of our belongings found their own spot in our house, matching as harmoniously as if we had acquired it all together. We were partners even before we met. In our almost five years living together, we jointly bought only one sofa. We had been so in tune with each other, so in love and excited about the future together. Now I was taking back to New York everything I'd brought—my Italian love seat, my dining table, my Westin Heavenly mattress, acquired after a conference at a Westin hotel, where everyone was obsessed with how well they slept the night before. The possessions of a single woman. I was leaving with my stuff as if I had just ended a long visit. The weight of what was about to happen hit me one day in yoga class as I lay on my mat trying to dissolve . . . I was leaving Jim.

I drove back to the house from the class tense and tired and found Eddie alone. No barking this time since he welcomed some company, only a sniff and a snort. I remembered Jim and the kids were going to Old Navy to shop for T-shirts. I fixed myself a sandwich and sat at the kitchen table with sections of the Sunday *Times* spread before me. From the corner of my eye I could see Eddie debating whether to chance it and try to get under the table. We made eye contact. I looked at him and he held my gaze—so innocent, so single-minded, so loyal, so present, so constant, so much like home—and so out of my life in just a matter of weeks.

I heard the garage door, and Eddie rushed to intercept Jim and the kids as they walked in with their shopping bags. Then I heard Jim.

"I know, I missed you too. You thought we'd never come back, did you? IknowIknowIknow."

I felt like crying.

Ten

Eddie and the City

left California and for a while felt disoriented. I missed Jim so much. I moped around New York as a "married single." But the city soon swallowed me and I barely found time to talk to my husband on the phone every night, let alone mourn over our tentative separation. I started the environmental beat at the *Times* for the Metro section and immediately was consumed with learning about a wide range of topics, from climate change to the toxic chemicals used by "organic" dry cleaners. As I waited out my tenants' lease so I could return to my apartment uptown, I rented a studio apartment from a colleague close to Times Square and the office. I had friends to reconnect with. I returned to old habits like theater on weeknights. This was my belief:

if you're going to put up with the hassles of New York, you'd better take advantage of what's unique about the city. As one of playwright Terrence McNally's characters says, without theater New York would be Newark.

While I was in L.A., the *Times* building had moved. It was no longer in the middle of the theater district, next to Times Square and Sardi's. Now it was on the outskirts two and a half blocks south, across from the Port Authority. The brand-new tower by Renzo Piano was too beautiful and too corporate for us ink-stained wretches, but everyone appreciated being even a tiny bit farther from the tourist hordes lining up for pictures with the Naked Cowboy.

I made it to New York just in time to watch Barack Obama become president, from the living room of my friend Dana, who had gathered neighbors and friends to watch election results. Jim watched from Tom and Sally's, our friends who hosted the pot-smoking lunchtime salons. Regardless of political affiliation, people at our bicoastal parties appreciated the historic moment.

After I left, Jim got a job with the L.A. bureau of Bloomberg News, covering finance and Wall Street in the middle of the financial crisis. We got back to the monthly-visit schedule. Sometimes we saw each other more frequently, even on consecutive weekends one time, because of our friends Bill and Scout's wedding in Palm Springs. The life changes kept coming as we came and went. Arielle started applying to colleges on the East Coast and eventually got accepted at a liberal-arts college in Maryland. She'd be only a few hours away from New York by bus and train. Henry became a dedicated rock and roller, playing drums in rock and jazz bands at school. At some point the decision was made that he would benefit from a more focused environment and would do best at a boarding school before moving on to college. Jim was deeply saddened as his nest emptied but was proud of his kids' growing independence. And he could now start thinking about his own move to join me in New York. He would be able to transfer to Bloomberg News's headquarters in New York. We'd experience New York together for the first time as a married couple, with the security of good jobs and the well-being of the kids taken care of. I couldn't believe it. And Eddie? I was still plotting.

While apart, Jim e-mailed daily with reports from the home front. Eddie's happy world had turned a bit fraught after Jim got the Bloomberg job and stopped working from home. No more five walks a day for Eduardo. Instead, Jim walked him before and after work and hired kids from the neighborhood to take him out in between. One of them was only forty pounds heavier than the dog.

"Baby, major thumbs-up on Day One of the dog walking!" Jim reported via e-mail. "After our conversation I was suddenly nervous about Eddie breaking free when he got to the house of his nemesis, but Lauren (who weighs about eighty pounds) said she was ready for his tricks and the moment passed without incident. Now I just have to remember whether I told her he likes to eat pugs . . ."

He signed off with "XXOO, Jaime"—James in Spanish.

Eddie could occasionally demonstrate a knack for self-preservation, so he behaved for this new transition. But it was too late for amends. I refused to see spots in my future, so we still needed to figure out what to do with him. A husband and a dog in a small apartment was a recipe for divorce. No belated showing of good faith on Eddie's part was going to steer me away from my resolve to use this life change as an opportunity to get rid of him. This was my only shot. His exit would be planned in a way that looked after his own interest. This was not going to be cruel or harmful to Eddie. Nothing like the dangerous situations he had put *himself* in many times.

He had more lives than a cat. Before I moved to California, he took off after a deer and disappeared for hours in the coyote-infested canyon after Jim let him off the leash on the trail behind his old town house. Somehow he made it back to the trail uninjured. Another time we left him in the care of the ex to go to Puerto Rico and he bolted during a walk. He reappeared in Venice Beach, at the home of another dog owner, who picked him up and called the number on his tag.

"I have your dog," the guy said in a voice mail. What a relief.

Making him disappear in a humane way would require a more concerted effort.

"Wouldn't Eddie be happier staying behind?" I asked my husband repeatedly. "He'll go crazy in a smaller place." A California dog, I argued, would not appreciate wintry, overcrowded, and cramped New York. I was lobbying for leaving him behind with friends or, as a second option, finding him a suitable home in New York, outside the city, where we could still visit him and he could still roam and chase squirrels to his heart's content. A farm, perhaps? He'd be so much happier in the country. Win-win. I asked anyone within earshot if they knew of options for our dog.

"What kind of dog is he?" someone asked at my friend Lynda's birthday dinner.

As I held the attention of about eight women at the round table, I couldn't stop myself and launched into my long list of complaints. When I was finished, we all agreed I shouldn't be the one to write the want ad.

"You will find no takers for 'spiteful dog that sheds and pees when scolded and may bite,'" one of the women noted.

I tried not to sabotage my search as I continued making inquiries among friends. I urged Jim to help with my placement efforts, but he resisted.

"I'm open to the idea if a good situation could be found," he said over the phone from California. "New York is where I'll be moving because you're there and New York is the center of the media world, and that's where I need to be. I have to look at my life and be a bread-winner for the family. I assumed I'd figure out a way to make him figure in my plans, but it'd be complicated. You hate the dog, you're pushing me to get rid of him. You said under no circumstances he'd be allowed in your apartment. It's not like I have a thousand options."

Wait—was that a yes or a no?

It was a no. I should have known my husband wouldn't budge.

"Eddie is part of our family," he declared, and that was that. Jim would not give Eddie up.

A few months after that conversation, on a glorious evening, the phone rang in my office. It was Jim, calling from Newark Airport.

"I made it. I can't wait to see you, darling."

Finally, the long-distance marriage was coming to an end. My husband and I were finally together in New York for good.

As I waited for our reunion, I couldn't even picture Eddie, who had been shipped in his crate on Jim's plane, in the city. This was going to be a disaster, I was sure. Already Jim was delayed because he had to pick up Eddie in the cargo area. An hour went by. He had arranged for a van to take them to the city from Newark. Where were they?

I called him.

"Where are you?"

"Eddie is stuck. The guy who's supposed to get him out of the plane apparently took a break."

Great. Dog trouble before the dog had even been unleashed here. I called Sazón, the Latin fusion restaurant in Lower Manhattan where I had planned to take Jim on his first night in the city, and canceled the reservation. I was still in the office, where there was always plenty to do, so I kept busy for another hour or so. I was about to bug Jim again, as it got closer to nine p.m., when he called to say he'd already checked in to the corporate apartment near Madison Square Park where Bloomberg News was putting him up for a few months. The plan was for me to move in with him from my own temporary quarters while my tenants in the apartment in the Heights moved out and I repainted and got it ready for us.

Jim and I arranged to meet somewhere in the West Thirties on Sixth Avenue.

As I headed south, I struggled with my bag of clothes and two bottles of wine. It was always rush hour in Midtown and the throngs were moving fast toward subway stops and nearby Penn Station. I muscled through to West Thirty-seventh Street and calculated Jim would soon be approaching me as he walked north. And then I saw them.

In the evening chaos, I first saw four legs in a sea of twos, and Eddie's blotched head looking every which way as he tried to keep up with all the stimuli. Eddie walked ahead of Jim as usual with a brisk step, fading in and out between the legs of pedestrians, as if he knew where he was going. It was an absurd image—Eddie in the city. My city. He belonged in this environment as much as a chicken on a leash. My thoughts immediately went to worst-case scenario—would he take a bite of one of the legs? But all worries momentarily dissipated when I looked up and saw my smiling husband, the picture of cheerful resiliency. We embraced under a sidewalk construction shed, by a life-size poster of Julianna Margulies advertising the new season of *The Good Wife*.

"Welcome to New York, baby!"

"Hi, darling," Jim said into my hair.

When Eddie saw me his tail waved, but he made no actual move to greet me. His eyes darted around and took in his new surroundings. Distance had not exactly turned him into Mr. Lovey-dovey. But not even Eddie could dampen my excitement. My hubby was home. We didn't linger on the sidewalk, as we were at risk of being swept away by the human tide. I traded my heavy bag for Eddie. I sensed his anxiety. He was usually nervous around groups of people; how was he going to cope with the legs, and the honking, and the sirens, and the assault on his senses from all directions? How was he going to avoid being trampled or run over? How was he going to survive gray days, snow, and winter? More important, where could I possibly let him go right now?

I realized that I had no clue what the etiquette was for dogs in New York. The sidewalks were cluttered with people, newsstands, and vendors. Every few steps, there was a building or store entrance. There was no grass, no bushes, only concrete. There were lampposts and hydrants, but also so many eyes watching. I didn't want to be yelled at by a doorman or a busybody. Fortunately, Eddie was too excited and distracted for his dog-walking routine. His sense of smell was on overdrive. He sniffed with his head tilted upward—Pretzel? Hot dog? Pizza? All of the above?—and his internal GPS could barely keep up. We walked by a deli with its glass doors wide open, a long salad-bar spread straight ahead. Eddie squared off in front of it, body upright like a soldier, ears and tail up at attention. He didn't move a hair as he assessed whether this apparition was real. I kept him on a short leash at heel position but had to tug hard to bring him back to earth. Jim was also tense.

"Don't let him walk on the grating," he said, pointing at the metal sidewalk grates that ventilated the subway tunnels underneath. "He hates it."

But I could tell Eddie loved New York. He wasn't cringing. He was engaged. How could I have ever doubted it? The streets were filthy, full of nibbling possibilities. The smells were overwhelming. (Eddie did not eat his dry food for four days after his arrival, though. The six-hour cross-country trip had traumatized him. "When he got out of the crate at the airport, he had this crazed look in his eyes," Jim said.)

When we got to the apartment building, Eddie had another first—his first elevator ride, all the way to the thirtieth floor. He saw a dog in the hallway when the doors opened on the fifth floor. When the doors opened again, this time on the tenth floor, Eddie was ready to "interact," but where did the dog go? Eddie let out a whimper as he relaxed his stance.

The corporate one-bedroom apartment was modern, spacious, and very white—walls, tile, counters, furniture. And, miracle of miracles, it was pretty quiet. But it was tiny compared to our house. There would be little room for Eddie to maneuver, since he would be immediately banned from the bedroom and bathroom. That left him with the kitchen and living room, about half the place, but still about the size of one of our bedrooms in the Palisades.

But he stayed true to his bad habits. When we came back from a late dinner, we found Eddie on the sofa.

"Don't do that, mister," Jim said as he shooed his dog off the cushions.

We could see the depression on the sofa and I put my face to it to count the hairs. Dozens! Eddie averted my eyes but I yelled at him anyway and he slinked away. I knew I'd have to police him all over again. I'd have to close the doors to the bedroom and bathroom, set sofa cushions upright, and put newspapers and bag packs on the sofa and chair. Every day we'd have to go through the same drill.

But I thought this was the perfect time to create new habits. I wanted to take advantage of his disorientation to get him used to sleeping in the crate. Why not? That was his routine when I first met him at Jim's town house, and he was happy. Eddie had other ideas.

That first night, he banged and banged against the crate. I was determined to use the Ferber method parents use to get babies to sleep. You comfort every so often, then you go back to bed and repeat until someone gives up. Jim just wanted Eddie to stop.

I persisted. "Dogs are creatures of habit," I told Jim, who seemed ready to throttle me but didn't say anything. "He'll get used to it."

I had earplugs (for snores, for sleeping on planes, to block out cell phone chatterboxes) and offered a pair to my husband. Another creature of habit, he declined. I fell asleep, but woke up to banging noises. I got up to go to the bathroom and found the crate halfway to the bedroom. I pushed it back to its corner. "Stop that!" I whispered.

All I could see were his two saucer eyes—two shiny black pools in the back of the crate, out of reach. I came back to bed and Jim was at his wit's end.

"He's obsessed. He won't stop. He's been doing that for four hours straight. I haven't been able to sleep."

"Okay, okay." I was at my wit's end too. This mutt wanted what he wanted. "What do you want to do?"

"Let him out so he can sleep on his bed."

I said nothing and Jim got up and let him out.

"Hope that's the last we hear of him," I said.

Scratch-scratch-scratch.

We were so tired we fell asleep to the rhythmic paws on the door as Eddie, having had one victory, was going for a second. It wasn't like we could open the door, move his cushion next to our bed, and call it a day. Some friends slept with their dogs that way and I could make an allowance just this one time for traumatized Eddie. But Eddie couldn't be trusted. There was no doubt that, once in the bedroom, he would try to get into our bed. Then he'd put his powerful butt to work and gradually push me off. He wanted to snuggle up with Jim, not me. He wanted to take my place. The next morning we found him waiting on the other side of the door, licking his paws from all the action the previous night.

Alas, there would be no honeymoon period in New York. Once again, Eddie and I would fight to see who was top dog.

Eddie fell head over heels for New York the moment he found a paper bag with chocolate chip cookie crumbs in the bushes during his first walk near Madison Square Park. He wouldn't pee on hard pavement, though, forcing us to always be on the lookout for a hedge. And New York—a city that managed to accommodate eight million people and their six hundred thousand dogs (compared to five hundred thousand cats)—adored dogs. As my friend Bruce complained one night over drinks at his watering hole, the Knickerbocker: "You go home with the woman and you first have to walk their dog."

As with humans, New York was particularly great for dogs if you had money—and were not embarrassed to do things like stand in a long line to order the Pooch-ini, vanilla custard with peanut butter sauce and a dog biscuit ("not intended for small dogs") from Shake Shack, the popular gourmet burger chain. No time for lines? Pet food stores delivered. Busy New Yorkers also paid for dog nannies and doggie day care. And the really wealthy paid professionals to teach their dogs to act humanlike in order to get past co-op boards and be able to buy their multimillion-dollar apartments. Among the lessons: no barking when the doorbell rings, no aggressive sniffing in lobbies and elevators, no paws on mink coats.

Wouldn't it be easier to just forgo the dog in the first place?

But a city this dense had its share of dog haters too. New Yorkers were jealous of their space and they wouldn't make concessions for dogs. The bitching was, of course, directed at dog owners—specifically, the kind who blocked your path with long leashes or an impromptu dog meet-and-greet with other ditzy owners, or who added to the city's stench of urine by letting the dog go in the middle of the sidewalk and on the side of buildings, or who brought dogs into subway cars (seriously, because the subway is not crowded enough?). It goes without saying that an owner who doesn't scoop would sooner or later be confronted. I had witnessed such arguments many times. New Yorkers could take only so much.

Mindful of the tensions, I told Jim we needed to learn fast how and where to walk Eddie. Where was a suitable place for a New York dog to relieve himself? With so much outdoor peeing going on in the absence of backyards, there had to be a long list of do's and don'ts.

But when we checked with friends they all seemed surprisingly blasé. Some friends were shockingly loose with the rules.

"Don't make eye contact," advised our friend Robert, who let his two schnauzers loose while walking them off-leash (against city law) in the Gramercy Park area. If someone happened to be watching, Robert told us, he pretended to scold the dogs. Robert also advised not to sit at the outdoor tables of restaurants closest to the sidewalk.

"My dogs pee on those all the time," he said.

I hated that Jim listened and nodded, as if he needed more encouragement to let Eddie be Eddie. He took Robert's advice to heart while I dutifully checked with the ASPCA website for advice on urban dog etiquette. It said no soiling a building entrance. It also advised to use the freight elevator or back exits when coming out of the apartment and to hurry through lobbies.

I was also going to follow the advice of friends who said trash bags piled high on the curb awaiting pickup were off-limits (although discarded Christmas trees seemed to be fair game), and so were building walls. Of course restaurant chairs and tables were a no-no too. I finally learned what "curb your dog" means—on the street next to the curb. You were supposed to walk the dog to the curb or edge of the sidewalk to do his business on the street—not mid-sidewalk, not on the trees or planters or stoops.

Jim and I made another discovery: cold, soulless New Yorkers who'd walk over you if you were slumped on the sidewalk motionless turned friendly and chatty at the sight of a dog.

"He's a chick magnet!" Jim happily reported after his first outings with Eddie.

When it was my turn to step out with Eddie on Sixth Avenue and walk toward Madison Square Park, I struggled more with keeping him away from the crap he shouldn't eat. The city was cleaner than ever but there were still plenty of food scraps strewn about. We got to the park, which I knew a little because of its proximity to a favorite Indian restaurant, Tabla, on Madison Avenue.

It is a gorgeous little urban park with red oaks and little-leaf linden trees and lots of American elms. We passed a playground and a lawn with an exhibit of monumental sculptures, but Eddie was laser-focused on the Shake Shack restaurant at the corner. He pulled me toward the delicious smells, but I tugged back because I was not about to let him make me pick up after him in front of an audience who was also just about to eat dinner. I was not joining the line to shell out four dollars for the Pooch-ini either. A dog run beckoned nearby, but Eddie didn't do dog runs (please refer to both the pug-eating incident and the kerfuffle with the cancer-ridden dog in chapter 5). It was a shame that Eddie was so antisocial because, from the rules posted outside the gate, there were worse things a dog could be.

"If your dog digs a hole, fill it before you leave," read one. Eddie was a lot of things but he was no digger (not yet, anyway).

We finally stopped in a sandy area by some bushes, not far from where four men sat on grass cross-legged in a circle, meditating. "Go to town, Eddie."

Eddie did less well indoors. The close quarters were too confining. I saw him get up from his bed, look around, and plop right back down after weighing the prospects. To make matters worse, every sound was a loud crash to his sensitive ears. For the first time, Eddie became scared of the dishwasher. We turned it on and he became hyper, wouldn't sit, climbed on us. We rubbed him or held him to calm him down, but we still needed clean dishes.

And he, of course, barked at every footstep in the hallway outside our door.

"Stop that," Jim commanded. "You're a city dog now."

Jim considered a bark collar, but we decided it was too much torture for such a temporary need. Meanwhile, his paws on the parquet floor sounded like Savion Glover on Broadway.

So many firsts for Eddie. I almost felt sorry for him.

No more sunbathing in the backyard, no more twisting on his back on the grass. No carpet to buff his coat with paws up in the air while we had dinner. No mail carrier to bark at. City living had its trade-offs, after all.

For weeks he continued to act strange. One night, when Jim couldn't stand the whimpering outside our bedroom door, he took him down thirty floors for a midnight walk. But the whimpering continued until Jim gave him an ultimatum in harsh tones. Eddie was not used to harsh words from Jim. He got the message and finally went to sleep.

One bright spot for Eddie was getting his first professional walker. After the neighborhood kids in the Palisades who charged five dollars per walk, Eddie became the charge of Amanda, a young woman from a dog-walking service that charged twelve dollars per fifteen-minute walk with another dog. Jim told Amanda that Eddie would go out only with submissive females. That's right. Just what New York's singles scene needed—another asshole.

On Amanda's first day, Jim left her a note on the kitchen counter. "Hi, Amanda. Thanks for walking Eddie. He loves people but is finicky around other dogs. Watch him closely. Please let me know how he does and we'll talk later."

"Hello," Amanda wrote back on the same piece of paper. "Wow! Eddie's a cool dog. He peed today!"

Easy-to-impress Amanda left cheerful notes signed with a heart one day, a happy face the next. When I met her, I asked her professional opinion about etiquette. She acted like she had never given it a passing thought.

"Pee is supposed to be bad for trees," she said. She scrunched up her face, trying to think of other rules. Apparently there were none except for common sense. "As long as you pick up, no one says anything," she said. "Obviously, you want to keep him away from merchandise."

Obviously.

Amanda and Eddie got along super.

"Eddieboy peed and it turned out to be a beautiful day," said another Amanda-gram left on the kitchen counter.

And they kept coming.

"Eddie did great with Eloise. They got along like old pals. He only peed. Didn't like any of the bushes we tried, I guess."

Jim also found his groove walking his mutt first thing in the morning and last thing at night.

Eddie seemed to be quite the sensation in Madison Square Park, according to his biased owner.

"Eddie's got a dog walker. He walks with a little dog named Eloise. He's sweet on Eloise. Life is good," Jim said one night while we watched TV.

The relocation, I had to admit, was going better than I ever imagined. My poor, battle-worn husband was breathing easy—until day ten. On this day Amanda reported that you-know-who just tried to get a chunk of Eloise. Nothing serious, though, so he wasn't dumped.

The next day Jim left Amanda a note. "Amanda, are you still walking Eddie with Eloise? How's that going?"

"Fantastic," she wrote back on the same piece of paper. "She's out of town 'til next week, so he's flying solo for now. Also walking with Truffles, another little female, also out of town. He peed."

Thank God for rich New York City dogs with second homes in the Hamptons.

But Jim and I would soon be moving into our permanent apartment and we needed to find the right kennel for our peculiar dog. After much discussion, Jim and I had agreed to house hunt in New Jersey, where we could afford to live. He wanted a house for Arielle and Henry to call home. I was okay with this as long as we also kept my apartment. Jim tried to get me to consider the money we'd save by having just one household. It was an added expense, for sure, but I had reasons for wanting to keep a foothold in the city. We both worked in Manhattan and would make use of the apartment whenever we stayed in the city until late for work or fun. I also pictured us old and retired with this second home, spending winters in warm weather and coming back to the apartment for four or five months of the year. I was thinking about convenience, and that if we sold we'd be forever priced out.

Some of my girlfriends were suspicious.

"You just don't want to be married," said Dana.

If anything, it was just the opposite. The apartment would certainly help the marriage if we found each other at odds again over the kids. I recognized that I was afraid or unable to give up that last part of the old me because the situation at home was often more complex than I was able to handle. I believed we were still working without a playbook. A refuge could still come in handy, with the added benefit that it would also be the ultimate Eddie-free zone.

"You're like Carrie and Mr. Big in the *Sex and the City* movie," said Taja-Nia, a member of my book club.

"It's not like that at all," I said.

In that movie, Mr. Big suggested spending a couple days a week apart—with one of them staying in Carrie's old apartment, the other one in their new luxurious one—so that they could pursue their own interests without feeling marriage was cramping their style. But for the most part, Jim and I would be together in either place. I knew Jim worried that I'd be spending more time in the city than in the house. He wasn't thrilled about the thought of spending any time apart again after the long-distance marriage. So we picked at least two firm city days—Wednesdays and Fridays—and the rest of the week we would go to the house in New Jersey. Eddie, however, would be restricted to the house and Jim would pay for extra walks when we were in New York. Now, more than ever, I didn't want our uncooperative psycho mutt to go anywhere near the new apartment. He had failed his first New York City test—living tight.

This was as good a compromise as any, although it still gnawed at me that we could do without the house if there was no dog in the picture. The visits from Arielle and Henry would be so sporadic that we could easily accommodate them in the apartment. Let's face it. The house was really for Eddie.

"What do you want me to do?" Jim said when I needled him about having a house mostly for the dog. "He's a responsibility."

We started our search in Montclair, where many colleagues lived.

It would take a couple months to find the house, so Jim spent one weekend telling lies on the phone as he searched for the perfect temporary home for Eddie.

"He's a very sweet guy," he told one boarder as I read the paper across from him at the dinner table. "His vet thinks he's a cattle dog, an Australian heeler. He's short-haired, forty pounds, and nine and a half years old, but very active."

Pause. "Yes, he's up on all his shots."

Pause. "He's a neutered male but does have problems with alpha-type male dogs, but with other dogs he's generally okay."

I chuckled at all the double-talk. "Generally okay" meant it was a crapshoot; we all knew what "problems" meant.

"I hope to visit him on weekends, take him out for walks," Jim said.

When he hung up, Jim looked at me wistfully, as if dreading the separation. For a second I wondered if he looked that miserable when I left California. He settled on Hal Wheeler's pet hotel, canine salon, and grooming academy in the Jersey town of Cedar Grove, which charged thirty-nine dollars a day but gave a ten percent discount for thirty days or more.

"They'll take good care of him, baby," I reassured him.

My upcoming Eddie-free vacation put me in a great mood. I looked forward to sleeping full nights for a change and coming home to a normal-looking sofa, with cushions where they belonged. Once Eddie was in his new temporary home, we moved to the apartment in Washington Heights and it felt like I was finally in our New York home. The Hudson and the George Washington Bridge were as majestic as ever. Mike, the night doorman, had much gossip about my neighbors and my former tenants. The hood had come up, with new restaurants and a spiffed-up liquor store that now held wine tastings, a sure sign of gentrification even in upstate Manhattan.

We eased into our cozy home. I planned to have the kitchen redone, as soon as we got the house, to accommodate more cooking, since Jim was such a good chef. Our daily commute was a cinch—a twenty-minute straight shot to our Midtown offices on the express A train. Cab fare from Midtown was now almost thirty dollars with tip, up by almost eight dollars since I left, so we took the subway even when we stayed out late. On the way home, we were usually in the company of musicians from Broadway shows carrying their cellos, saxophones, and big basses after the theater let out.

I didn't miss Eddie, but Jim longed for him in the worst way. "I miss my scoundrel."

The first reports back from the kennel were that Eddie was not eating. When we visited him the first weekend, Jim worried that Eddie would be mad at him and not forgive him. As we waited, a screen in the lobby showed the area where the dogs were kept. The confines were roomy and the dogs could see one another through the chain-link cages. Jim handed an attendant Eddie's leash and a few minutes later a door opened and Eddie appeared, pulling at the leash toward us. He sniffed us, jumped up Jim's leg, sneezed a few times, and seemed elated to see us. He wagged his tail forcefully, butt in full swing. He even jumped up to greet me with paws on my belly and snuck a lick on the tip of my nose—a first! I was relieved to see him so happy. We took him to the car for an outing in a park nearby and he whimpered in the backseat, trying to get to the front seat between us.

"Sit, Eddie, sit!" I commanded, but instead he licked my face.

Jim looked just as excited, steering with one hand and scratching his buddy with the other. "Did you give her a big, wet kiss?" he asked the dog. "Poor guy. He's lost in the world. Soon enough, Eddie, soon enough."

I noticed something. "His paws are orange. Why is that?"

We couldn't figure it out. Eddie was also noticeably thinner.

We drove to a trail popular with dogs in the vicinity of the kennel. The afternoon was cold and it was drizzling, but Jim and Eddie were happily oblivious to the weather. When we got back to the kennel, there was no drama. Eddie went up the entrance steps eagerly, as if recognizing the place as his new home.

We asked about the raw paws and the keeper at the kennel told us they were orange from all the pacing dogs did while caged. I felt bad, but not bad enough to change my mind and bring Eddie with us to the apartment. Jim fed Eddie a biscuit from a jar on the counter and we said our good-byes. When the attendant came for him, Eddie went willingly. No whimpers.

I gained more respect for Jim's bond to his dog during those visits. I saw true love in their reunions.

"I just miss having my buddy around," Jim said back in the car.

"What do you miss?"

"He wags his tail. He never talks back. He thinks my ideas are brilliant. He laughs at my jokes."

Ouch.

Jim understood the hassles we avoided by having Eddie tucked away. But he felt it made life more difficult just the same. "There's six more things to do," he said.

And, like your typical unreasonable dog owner, he was in denial. Eddie being a pest in the Bloomberg News apartment, he was convinced, was just a reaction to being in unfamiliar surroundings after the trauma of cross-country flying. Things would be different in our apartment. "He would be perfectly behaved," he told me with a straight face. "He's our dog and he should be with us in our living space."

I was not without empathy, but no. As we left Hal Wheeler's in the distance, I tried to lighten the mood. "Is this your way of saying I should wag my tail more?"

"Among other things."

I kissed my husband's lips. We were good, mostly because even in his temporarily resentful state, Jim knew I was resigned to coexist with my nemesis. Their separation anxiety would last only a few months, after all. My cross to bear looked indefinite.

Eleven

New Beginnings
(A Dog Gets Old)

Eddie had been the constant in Jim's life as everybody else relocated away from him. I was the first one to leave. While we were separated, Jim took Henry to his boarding school. He left him with a heavy heart after spending days meeting teachers and other students and their families, familiarizing himself with his son's new surroundings. And after taking Arielle to visit colleges, he took her to her new school in Maryland, where he got to know her roommates and shopped with her at Target for everything from comforters, sheets, and pillows to toothpaste, shampoo, and rugs. Then he moved to New York. With just the two of us, and Eddie, we no longer had to whisper when we argued.

I felt for Jim and recognized the importance of his dog—his spotted rock—through the rites of passage. Eddie was still the same Eddie, though, so while my husband looked for a convenient location to the city as we went house hunting, I looked for houses with a layout that could be easily dog-proofed. I used my veto power wisely, narrowing down the choices to houses with features that facilitated keeping Eddie contained and away from me—such as two floors and a staircase that could be gated. It didn't take long to find the perfect place on the southern edge of Montclair. The house was an Arts and Crafts–style four-bedroom, like a William Morris cottage, with rusticated brick outside and chestnut wood trim. Nice backyard, ample closet space, great fireplace and, best of all, a door to the upstairs. An Eddie-free floor at last.

Montclair was a liberal oasis surrounded by mostly white, mostly Republican towns where residents used McCain/Palin signs as porch décor. Leafy, pro-Obama/Biden Montclair, with its racially diverse population of about forty thousand residents, was particularly popular for its good schools and short commute to New York's Penn Station and the Port Authority.

Half the New York media world—and Stephen Colbert—went home to Montclair. We had so many friends and acquaintances there who worked for the *Times*, Bloomberg News, *The Wall Street Journal*, and other news outlets, I worried that I would have to hide in the ethnic foods aisle at Kings food market to avoid being seen shopping without makeup in my sweats. Most restaurants in Montclair were BYOB and nicely casual. Montclair State University presented A-list music and dance shows for fifteen dollars a pop. Our neighbors put on a block party every year. What's not to love?

The commute by trains and buses, that's what. You had to deal with fixed schedules and not-so-frequent rides. On weekends, the train to Montclair ran every two hours instead of hourly as it did during the workweek. The subway, by contrast, ran every ten minutes or less, depending on your timing. The pace of the burbs didn't slow us down as much as it required us to become better planners and more efficient. That was a bit of a challenge for a certain someone who lived up to the Latino stereotype—I was always late.

But we took to our new surroundings in no time, and so did Eddie.

The day we moved in, Jim went to spring Eddie free from the kennel. He came back beaming like a proud papa. The report card for "Eddie Sterngold" was impeccable, as it befitted a dog kept fenced in, away from other dogs and under constant watch with surveillance cameras.

The card read:

Temperament: "Friendly. Outgoing. Happy."

Appetite: "Good."

General Health and Appearance: "Good."

Additional Comments: "Eddie did very well in the kennel. Happy and social. He will be missed by the staff."

With any luck, the staff wouldn't be missing him for too long and would see him often.

I read somewhere to be mindful of how to introduce a dog to a new house. You are not supposed to let the dog loose in the house so he could check it out on his own and feel like he was in charge. When Eddie came home, I had him sit outside the front door in the screened-in porch while Jim and I went in first. We came out and put him on the leash and I took him inside, from room to room, only downstairs, giving him the message that I was granting him permission to be in the house, that I was in charge. The memories of our first day in the Palisades still stung. But my controlled tour was such a failure that I was soon buying plastic sofa and chair covers—and an alarm that gave out piercing beeps whenever it sensed motion from a spotted dog—to keep Eddie in check. (Plastic seemed more upscale than boxes and books.)

While I customized our new house, Jim picked a new dog walker. It was important to find one who could take care of Eddie overnight when we stayed in the city, or who would at least drive him to the kennel and back if need be. The lucky gal was Karin, who like all other walkers and sitters, had to go through a hazing to show her mettle.

It all started sweetly enough.

"Eddie pooped for me today. K.," read the first note on the kitchen counter.

She had the habit of giving Eddie a biscuit at the end of each walk.

"Bye, Eddie. I love you," I overheard her saying to her client. "See you tomorrow. Have a good afternoon."

Another day, another note.

"Pooped again today. I guess he likes me."

And another one: "Hi, Jim. Eddie pooped for me. May I take a picture of Eddie and use it on my website?"

Wait for it, wait for it.

Three weeks in, Karin kept Eddie overnight and he bit two other dogs she was boarding, a black Lab and some kind of terrier, both bigger than he was.

"Don't know what happened," she told us. "He just went after them last night and this morning. No big deal. I just separated them."

But when Eddie did it again during another stay, sweet Karin said enough. What she actually said, extremely apologetically, was: "I'm really sorry things did not work out at my house."

Seasoned dad that he was, Jim understood. He left Karin Godiva milk chocolates on the kitchen counter.

"The chocolates are from Eddie," the note read.

Then he asked me: "What's the canine equivalent of a misanthrope?"

Overnight stays were rare, though. We needed the walker mostly for midday, while we were both at work in Manhattan. Eddie's routine was pretty much what it was in L.A. A walk with Jim and a cupful of dry food in the morning. Repeat in the evening. New neighborhood meant new friends and foes. His first New Jersey friend was Linus the beagle.

"They were friendly and chewed on each other's necks a little bit," Jim reported after their first encounter. "It was very sweet."

Honey, a small setter and cocker spaniel mix, was love at first sight—Eddie peed three times while she was watching. Cody, some kind of terrier, a Westie or something, eventually became a friend also. But I was soon instructed to watch out for Daisy, some beige mutt. With no kids in the house, I had to pitch in more with dog-walking duties. The streets were mostly deserted when I walked Eddie and I usually checked e-mail on my phone while he meandered.

One morning, though, a guy startled us when he stopped his car in front of us.

"Is that a pit bull?"

My guard was up. It was hard to switch from my New York City state of mind. I was always on high alert for strangers on the street pretending to be friendly. Usually they just wanted money but I was once flashed by a pervert. I relaxed when I saw a four-legged passenger in the backseat panting and checking us out. The guy was either a dog lover or a dognapper. Either way, it was fine with me.

"No, he's a mutt."

"Oh, because he does look a little bit like a pit bull."

"Well, my husband says he's a mix of blue heeler and something else."

"He's one hundred percent pure beauty," the guy said, driving off as quickly as he appeared.

I told Jim about the encounter later that night.

"He was talking about you," my hubby said.

"Thanks, baby, but no, that's what's sad," I said. "Your dog, not your wife, stops traffic."

The world just revolved around the dog.

"Hope everything looks good," our twice-a-month housekeeper wrote on a note asking for stainless steel cleaner and Swiffer wet mopping cloths. "Eddie must not like the rain. He's in the doldrums this a.m.!"

Montclair allowed us a semblance of a California lifestyle, and Jim loved it. He could still mow the lawn and walk his dog at a leisurely pace along tree-shaded streets. And our house, on the border of Montclair and Glen Ridge, was seven-tenths of a mile from the nearest train station and bus stop. Jim biked to the station, happily pedaling with his briefcase in a front basket.

"Good-bye, Beaver!" I teased as he rode away.

I had to walk, and often ran if I was late along with the other laggards. At least we got the exercise. I managed to miss several annoyingly punctual trains before I was able to time my walks right.

The area had the feel to me of a weekend getaway more than home. Beautiful, peaceful, and not so boring. We had Russian spies! Soon after we moved in, news broke that an all-American-looking family living somewhere in Montclair had been caught in an FBI sweep that also snared a woman columnist for *El Diario La Prensa*. Kind of exciting. The case even inspired the FX drama *The Americans*.

Montclair was not the wild reserve the Palisades was, but there was still plenty of wildlife, including deer and coyotes. Eddie liked to loll about in our backyard, although there was not as much sunlight as there was in California. In the unpredictable, too-hot-or-too-cold East Coast weather, we seldom ate outdoors. Too many bugs too, although we loved the fireflies. Eddie resourcefully found a new pastime: digging. We were not sure what he was digging for, but we tried not to leave him to his own devices outdoors for too long.

Jim was also vigilant against a new potential hassle—Jersey squirrels. We read that squirrels didn't normally attack unprovoked, which meant they would bite and scratch the hell out of our provocateur. They seemed to travel in packs and they were not easily intimidated. In a typical encounter during one walk, Jim and Eddie turned the corner and a trio of squirrels stopped what they were doing to watch from the lawn of a house. They were just a few feet from Eddie, but they didn't scurry away. The three amigos were unflappable, Jim told me, and secure in their turf. They just stared him down, like Tony Soprano, and Eddie knew to move on.

Blotched-head, however, could be fearless when he should retreat. We discovered our dog was a stone-cold killer on a miserably hot summer night. It was ninety degrees and humid, and Jim was grilling on the back porch. Eddie was in and out, with the kitchen door open for a minute or two, as Jim tended to the chicken. All was well until Eddie shot past Jim like a rocket. Jim heard some strange growling, and by the time he looked up, Eddie was shaking his head with a skunk in his mouth.

"Drop it, drop it," Jim screamed, but it was too late.

The smell was overpowering.

Eddie kept shaking his head even with a dead skunk in his mouth. Jim was surprised his darling dog had not been just curious or aggressive—he'd set out to murder. But this was no time for reflection. He grabbed a plastic bucket and threw it at the dog, who finally dropped his prey. Now the real fun began. Eddie started to run toward the house, and Jim slammed the door shut before the dog could get in. He was licking himself, with all this goo on his face. Jim got the leash and tied Eddie to the metal handle on one of the storm doors below the porch, leaving him to hose the backyard down to dilute the smell. He shoveled the skunk into a garbage bag and that bag into another two bags and put it on the driveway. That's when he called lucky me. I happened to be staying at the apartment that night because of an early assignment in the city the next day.

"How the fuck do I treat this dog?"

I Googled "how to remove skunk smell from dog" and gave Jim a de-skunking recipe that included hydrogen peroxide, baking soda, and liquid soap. Jim didn't have all the ingredients, so he got in the car to drive to the store. He called me again.

"I suddenly have this vision that I'm going to get in the car, leave him tied up on the porch, and the skunks in the neighborhood are going to organize and attack him to get even for killing their friend."

"Baby, skunks are not coyotes," I said, not really knowing what I was talking about but fairly certain Jim was panicking and it was my job to calm him down. "Go get the stuff. Eddie will be fine."

Dinner was history. Jim stayed up until midnight making batches of the mixture and alternating between scrubbing Eddie in the driveway and flooding the backyard. He went to bed exhausted and hungry. When I came home the next day, I wondered if Eddie would be a blond. He wasn't. His spots had survived the hydrogen peroxide. But he stank for days. Skunks always have the last word.

I felt sorry for my husband, but I'm not going to lie—I was relieved I wasn't in the house for this particular dog drama. There are times that define who the real dog owner is, and this was one of them. Jim made so many other sacrifices for his mutt. When we stayed in the city overnight on Fridays, he had to rush back to Montclair on the eight a.m. train from Penn Station so he could walk and feed Eddie. That meant getting up at six-thirty a.m. on a weekend morning.

"I feel like the mistress," I told Jim every time he left me.

Even when the New York City Office of Emergency Management issued hazardous travel advisories for rain, snow, sleet, and locusts, Jim braved the mile-long walk or bike ride from the train station in Montclair to the house. He put himself in harm's way for this dog. He couldn't find sitters to feed Eddie in the morning. And if the entrance to the house was not shoveled, forget it—the sitters wouldn't come anyway, even if bribed with money and Godiva chocolates.

Such are the joys of dog ownership.

New York weather complicated everyone's lives, even the dog's. Eddie wasn't used to this East Coast hell in the summer, which made him lethargic. On the worst days, Jim had to leave the air conditioner on in the living room while we were at work.

Our first winter in Montclair, Eddie snapped back to his old self once temperatures started cooling. When it snowed, he didn't seem to mind. His nose could still detect smells. But the first time it got really cold, in the twenties, he cut his own walk short. He pulled on the leash toward the house mere minutes after I took him out. Jim gave walking another try and Eddie resorted to civil disobedience— he played dead and Jim had to carry him back to the house. He shivered indoors and came looking for extra warmth by sitting at my feet. I placed my hand on his head and it was vibrating. The heater was on, but he was freezing.

For the first time in a blue moon, I went shopping for the dog. I got him a green nylon coat with black reflective stripes, lined with fleece inside, on sale for eleven dollars. With the new orange collar Jim recently got him, he looked as well coordinated as Ralph Lauren's blue heeler. At the pet shop's checkout counter I had ignored booties for $39.99. Eddie was likely to hate them and bite them off the second after I put them on. But when I strapped the coat on him, he didn't fight it.

"Maybe we can wrap plastic around his paws and tie it with a rubber band as a test," I told Jim.

"He'd be embarrassed when he runs into his friends. He may be bullied."

"Well, I'm not spending forty dollars unless I'm sure he won't pull them off again."

After weeks of cold temperatures, Jim and I were looking forward to our annual escape to Puerto Rico for New Year's Eve. We kenneled Eddie and headed for the airport right after work on a Friday night. I called Mami as we waited at the gate, but she didn't pick up. This had become typical. My mom had reached the age of memory trouble and unexplainable quirks. Her new thing was to unplug anything plug-gable "to prevent fires." She had started losing short-term memory in her seventies, but, in her eighties now, she was still able to take care of herself and function normally enough to give me laughs and make me mad in equal parts. The only way to reach her lately was to call my sister so she could hand her cell phone over to our mother.

So I called my sister and went through the drill.

"Mami, you have to take the cordless phone with you wherever you are in the house. I've called and called, but you never answer it."

"What? But I haven't been out. When did you call?"

"Just now. And Tuesday, and Thursday."

"At what time?"

"At different times, Mami. You just don't hear it because you have it in the bedroom behind a closed door and you're watching television in another room. Or maybe it's unplugged."

"But I haven't been out. Let me check if there's a tone."

"No, Mami. Forget it. Just take it with you wherever you are."

"But I've been in the house and no one has called."

Oooooooooooooooommmmm.

I cut our conversation short as Jim and I boarded the plane.

"See you soon, Mamita," I said. I just wanted to hear her voice, just in case. I'd never completely lost my fear of flying. But it was a short hop to the island from New York, about four hours. Soon enough, Jim was looking at my hair with a grin.

"We must be close," he said.

It was an old joke. We were about to land in humid San Juan and my straight winter tresses had already started curling upward as we approached the airport. By touchdown, the top of my head was a for-est of frizz. We never needed the pilot to tell us we were on our final descent. When I began to look like Big Orphan Annie, it was time to put all electronics away. Growing up in tropical weather, this was the bane of my young life—every day was a bad hair day. On this trip, my carry-on contained bobby pins for the dubi-dubi—the trick of wrapping your hair around the crown of your head and pinning it tightly for a few hours to straighten the waves and curls. I also carried plenty of clips, barrettes, headbands, and elastic bands for further taming. It was all in vain.

When Jim and I visited Puerto Rico, we took time to both see family and vacation all around the island. We stayed in cute B&Bs or *paradors* in places like El Yunque's rain forest; Rincón, a surfers' hot spot on the island's west; and Vieques, a beach paradise off the coast of Puerto Rico where the United States Navy used to stage live-fire and bombing training exercises. My idea of bliss was to sit by the water with a book and a piña colada; Jim's was to be out in the water catching and releasing (also known as harassing) tarpon. But we always timed our annual visits to the main event: New Year's Eve. It was the biggest party of the year and it was a family affair. Older kids could go do whatever they wanted after midnight, but for the countdown you needed your loved ones with you. That meant parents and kids celebrated the new year together, mostly at house parties. Within my huge extended family on my mom's side—three brothers and seven sisters multiplied by children and grandchildren—New Year's Eve had been hosted at some relative's home or our own house in rotation. The bar was stocked with rum, whiskey, and homemade *coquito*, the rum-spiked coconut eggnog. The potluck food includes the traditional *pasteles*, *arroz con gandules*, *pernil*, and *guineitos en escabeche*, a fat-and-carb fest of plantain pies, rice with pigeon peas, pork shoulder, and green plantains in a vinegary marinade.

After that, only more sugar with our alcohol would do: *arroz con dulce* (coconut rice pudding), *tembleque* (a coconut gelatin that shakes like Jell-O), and guava paste with cheese. But nothing got eaten until we formed a circle to scream "*Diez! Nueve! Ocho! Siete! Seis! Cinco! Cuatro! Tres! Dos! Uno!* Happy New Year!" In the ensuing kissing and hugging, an aunt or two would peel off to sit by the radio and cry listening to the traditional *El Brindis del Bohemio*, a Mexican poem about a man's New Year's toast to his absent mother. Tears wiped off and dried, the buffet dinner would follow and the party would continue until two or three in the morning or until the last drunk stumbled out.

The party had shrunk considerably by the time Jim met me and joined in. The family had sustained departures—usually to the afterlife or Miami. In time, my extended family became even more so, scattered farther north and west in the States, in places like Atlanta, Dallas, and Corpus Christi. For this year's celebration, it was just Mami, my sister and nephews, and a friend or two and their families. My closest cousin, Ednita, was with her daughter in Orlando and other cousins were otherwise occupied, so we stayed home. We gathered on Mari's terrace upstairs. My sister cooked the traditional foods, and Jim and I took care of the liquor and refreshments.

But while there was plenty to eat and drink as the party got under way at nine p.m., no one was dancing. My sister and a girlfriend sat on the terrace chatting, the kids were running in and out with loads of firecrackers to set off on the street, and only my mom and I were trying to get into the spirit, with Jim pitching in as our salsa partner every other song with a frown. Jim was appalled that kids of all ages were handling fireworks on the street with little adult supervision. The kids were fine. It was the adults I worried about. It was common around the island for guns to go off at midnight. Even though they were pointed up, New Year's Day was a day of reckoning—revelers woke up hung over and bracing themselves for the news and the toll of people killed or injured by stray bullets.

But tonight Mami and I danced and danced to salsa and merengue music from the rocking party playing out on one of the island's television channels, oblivious to the deafening noise from the sky. My mom was just shy of her eighty-fourth birthday but she had a strong grip as she held me and a sure step when we separated to break it down. She was a little thin, and had diabetes and a touch of dementia, but her body still responded to the percussion of our African roots. When the song was jamming, she did a little jump and let out an "Ehee!" I laughed and wished with all my heart that dancing was the last thing to go for me too.

A few days later, Jim and I were on our way to pick up my mother to go to Costco when my sister called me to say that our mom had fallen in the bathroom. She was bent down, toweling off her legs, and when she straightened up she lost her balance and fell backward. My sister, who was always with her when she showered these days, caught her, but not before my mother hit her back hard against the tiled wall.

When we got to the house my mom was in pain but nothing seemed broken. We all thought she just needed some Advil and rest. Jim was leaving for New York the next day and when they said good-bye as she lay in bed my mom held his hand and told him in English: "I love you, Jim." The next day, she complained about excruciating pain so we took her to the emergency room, where they didn't find anything broken but sent her home with ultra-strong painkillers.

"Make sure she drinks a lot of water," the doctors told us.

Somehow, Mami began a steady deterioration that within days led her back to the hospital and, finally, renal failure. My sister and I didn't leave her bedside. We took turns covering her with kisses, telling her we loved her over and over, sitting by her side with our heads buried on her chest, feeling her heart. We put earphones on her so she could listen to salsa music on an iPod as her breathing became more labored. A nurse warned us not to talk about her condition within earshot.

"They can hear everything," she said.

We knew Mami could hear us and feel us because she waited for my sister and me to fall asleep next to her in a cot, and only then did she take her last breath.

Losing my mother so abruptly, exactly fourteen days after we'd danced, felt like she was killed in a car accident or some act of violence. I didn't think I had experienced real suffering until that day—not when my father died, not when my dear childhood friend and dance partner, Junior, died in his thirties after a long illness, not when a younger cousin was stabbed to death by her boyfriend, not when her brother, who was my age, later died of abdominal cancer. I didn't know what to do with myself. Whatever faith I had, it failed me. Where did you go, Mami? *¿Dónde estás?* Where are you? I tried to change the subject in my head so I wasn't pulled into a black hole of despair.

Regrets provided a huge distraction. I should have phoned my mother more. Our conversations had gotten shorter over time as she was losing her memory. She asked the same questions over and over and I usually began my good-byes after she'd asked me for the fifth time, "And how are things over there?" She could no longer catch me up about the neighbors or remember what my nephews were up to.

She wasn't able to share the latest shenanigans of local politicians or island celebrity gossip. I had been losing Mami in dribs and drabs. But she had not forgotten she was my mother. I still asked for her advice and she still listened to my whining about work or life with great interest. She was still the person who loved me the most, and she was the person I loved the most.

Dinorah Pérez de Navarro—mother, grandmother, wife, feminist, shopper par excellence, half of Las Chicas Marshall with her chum and *comadre* Josefina, *muchacha*, *salsera*, Rosita the riveter, my role model, my mommy—thank you for everything. The luck was all mine.

The emptiness Mami left behind was so overwhelming that I spent days hugging the walls whenever I thought of her absence. But I still had Jim, who didn't leave me alone one moment and who gave a lovely eulogy. And I still had my sister, who was stoic in her grief. I was grateful for all my cousins and relatives, and for my mom's girlfriends and the friends who gathered around us on a damp afternoon to watch my sister and I plant a silver buttonwood tree with Dinorah's ashes in her beloved garden.

Back in the States, I wasn't angry even if I felt the doctors could have done better. And I didn't feel sorry for myself, even when I was officially an orphan now. I eventually accepted my mom's death just as I became resigned to the aging going on all around me. Even the Lipsters, my circle of accomplished, ball-busting girlfriends, were talking about face-lifts. Like me, my friends were getting old, not just older. I didn't remember when exactly dinner conversations started veering to the latest weird shit that was happening to us, but our health was now a common topic.

My friends Michael and Leslie had a bad case of acid reflux. My friend Hector first battled some mandibular problem called TMJ, then was diagnosed with very treatable but still baffling tonsil cancer. My girlfriend Susan was hobbling around in major pain with sciatica. But my friend Robert won. We went to the Joyce Theater to see the flamenco dancer Soledad Barrio and over wine afterward he told me that he was having these strange coughing fits. The diagnosis: his tongue was too far back in his mouth. No kidding. Robert just learned this in his sixties.

"He told me my tongue is too far back," Robert said of the doctor, "and that there's nothing anyone can do about it." The news screamed for a second opinion, but the next doctor concurred—he told Robert the first doctor was reputable and he agreed with the diagnosis. Robert loaded up on sugarless cough drops and that was that.

I added "retracting tongue" to the list of what to look forward to in my golden years. But I already had my own woes to keep the medical industry busy. First, I got something called plantar fasciitis, a sharp pain on the sole of my right foot. I went to my internist, who referred me to a podiatrist, but not before she handed me a 1996 column by *Times* health columnist Jane Brody, who happened to sit next to me at the office! Jane wrote in her usual no-nonsense style that the condition was an inflammation of the ligament—the plantar fascia— that ran the length of the foot from heel to toes and could become disabling if ignored. It required stretching, massaging, and wearing a raised heel. The next time I saw Jane, I told her that she should collect my insurance co-payment from my doctor. I took comfort in the fact that plantar fasciitis afflicts athletes. Maybe I was exercising and walking too much? "No," the podiatrist said. "Just wear shoes with at least an inch or so of heel." No more cute flats for me. Ugly orthopedic shoes were surely next.

The pain in the foot gone, I looked in the mirror one morning and noticed that a couple of bottom eyelashes were growing inward. What in the world? Are they scratching the cornea? I went to the eye doctor and he said the cure for my condition was tweezers. A few months later, a pimple sprang up from the corner of my right eye (unrelated to either the wayward lashes or the tweezers). I was supposed to treat this with hot compresses or, as my other eye doctor suggested—and she wasn't joking—a potato heated in the microwave and wrapped in a towel. Sometimes I came out of my doctors' fancy Park Avenue and Upper West Side offices with the funny feeling that they were having fun at my expense.

Doctor #1: "Did she take the potato bit seriously?"

Doctor #2: "Yes. She even asked if she was supposed to get Yukon Gold or some other kind. HAHAHAHAHAHAHAAAA!"

Aging, as my friend Celia liked to say, was for the birds.

I guess I should have been grateful that my medical problems were minor, so far. Cancer was on my mind because of Hector and because Jim had just partnered up with Dr. Paul Marks, the longtime director of Memorial Sloan Kettering Cancer Center, to write Dr. Marks's memoir. We spent many dinners talking about his research for what would become *On the Cancer Frontier—One Man, One Disease, and a Medical Revolution*. I gained a deeper understanding of why there's no cure and why prevention and early detection were so critical to survival rates. What a crapshoot this longevity business was. Even if your body came through, the mind could say *"No más."* My beautiful cousin Alma—a poet, an eternal optimist, my confidante and all-time favorite human being—started showing signs of Alzheimer's in her fifties. By her sixties, we had taken away her car keys and, gradually, more and more of her old life and privacy until we moved her into a long-term-care home. She no longer recognized me or anyone else. Alzheimer's, which seemed to run on my mother's side of the family and afflict only the women, was a terrifying subject of conversation among my other female cousins.

"What are we going to do with ourselves when the time comes?" we asked each other.

We found some genetic reassurance among the aunts and uncles who were healthy septuagenarians, especially Titi Edda, the youngest of my mom's siblings. A mother, grandmother, and former actress, she still went out on dates and she was still the life of the party. She sang, she danced, she recited poems, she drank rum and Cokes, she reapplied lipstick to go get the mail.

"*Querida!*"—My dear!—she cried whenever she saw me, as dramatic as Norma Desmond in *Sunset Boulevard*. All anyone wanted was to be like her.

My father-in-law, Hank, a retired engineer and World War II veteran, was far ahead in the endurance race. At ninety, he went to the gym every day, traveled internationally, headed the architecture committee at his assisted-living place, and lived with a new, younger wife, Anita, who was in her seventies. Jim was very close to his dad and we kept track of all his adventures, hoping to emulate them. My elders taught me that money and mobility—and continued interest, curiosity, and engagement with the world—were what was required for the golden years to be truly golden.

But these people were freaks.

Nowhere did I gain more insight into our mortality, nowhere did I see more clearly where we were headed—all of us, inexorably, one by one, on the same slow-moving line—than in our lump-on-a-log. Eddie was now approaching his seventies, in dog years. He was officially a senior and it was starting to show. It wasn't like the seventies were the new fifties for dogs. He was limping some and was going deaf. He no longer met us at the door at the first jingle of the keys. Jim now stood in the kitchen jiggling the leash in vain, but no Eddie came barreling through to the kitchen knowing it was time for his walk. Jim had to go rouse him.

"Tsk-tsk, come on, big galoot."

Eddie and I no longer ran together. One day I put on my sneakers and said, "Okay, Eddie, we're going to jog." But we couldn't. We went out and I started jogging on the street, staying away from the tempting smells of the sidewalk, but Eddie was sluggish and slowing me down, which was really saying something. I ran at a turtle's pace. Eddie struggled to keep up and looked fatigued. He had lost it. We gave up running. It felt like the end of an era.

Eddie's personality, always weird, became weirder. He switched allegiances and now barked at Jim.

Gotcha! What really happened was that he was more cranky and clingy than ever. When we were alone and I worked upstairs in the office, I could hear him whimpering downstairs. He had separation anxiety just one floor away. It was difficult to hear the interviewee on the other end of the line, or concentrate on writing the story that was due in less than two hours, with Mary Magdalene acting up downstairs.

Eddie became irredeemably dense. He used to follow commands like staying away from the kitchen when we were cooking. Sometimes he'd walk the length of the kitchen to his water dish pretending to be thirsty, just to check what crumbs had fallen along the way, but normally he'd be patient and lie down nearby to watch us. Now I shooed him away and he came right back. I could do that ten times and ten times he'd forget to stay out. I moved his food and water bowls from the kitchen to the nook between the kitchen and the dining room so he didn't have an excuse to be in between our legs. No deal. He acted more and more like a senile grandpa, looking disoriented, as if he had no idea what we were talking about and didn't really care.

Now everything had to be looked at through the prism of possible senility.

Still, I couldn't help but be suspicious of Eddie's "deafness" or "limp" (only indoors) or "memory loss"—how convenient!—as yet another ploy to ignore my commands, do what he wanted, and get one more scratch. How could we know that this was really senility? I didn't totally buy into the idea Eddie was losing his marbles. He wasn't consistent enough to convince me yet. He hobbled and limped, sometimes all he lacked was shackles to look even more pathetic, but it could be all an act. The minute Jim appeared or mentioned "walk," Eddie was young again, galloping around like a pony.

The onset of Eddie's deterioration seemed to have happened overnight.

I realized just how feeble he had become on a Sunday afternoon. I was upstairs and heard paws on the steps. They were quiet paws, gingerly going up, getting closer and closer. I approached just as cautiously from my end to meet him at the top of the stairs and surprise him.

"Ha! Caught in the act!" I gloated. "Eddie! Go back down!"

He was positioned on two steps and had trouble turning around. When he tried, his body shook and he looked scared. It was as if he had forgotten how to walk down the steps, just like my Titi Alma. When I last visited her at her long-term-care home, she held on to me for dear life when we walked down a flight of stairs to go out to the garden. Her Alzheimer's advancing fast, she didn't remember how to do it anymore. I now contemplated Eddie with new regard for his growing frailty, and grabbed him by the collar.

"Okay, old galoot," I said, helping him down. "Let's do this together."

He was tentative, almost sitting before each step forward, but I didn't have to carry him. It was becoming harder to hate Old Eddie. He wasn't going to torment me forever. Eventually, he would be another loss. They said all that was left was the love. We had to share the man, why not the love too? It wouldn't be the first such three-some. I sometimes looked at Eddie and saw a cute, woolly pet with a purity of heart. He was usually asleep when this happened. Awake, Eddie couldn't help himself. We were set in our routines. Jim traveled regularly for events at Henry's and Arielle's schools, such as parents' weekend, and I stayed with Eddie. As usual, Eddie would instantly cozy up to me, only to turn against me or ignore me upon Jim's return. If there was a choice between saying hello to me in the morning or walking right past me to go park his butt somewhere new, it was always the latter. "Good morning, Eddie." Tepid tail wag, no licks, no nuzzle, not even a look. He was saving his energy. At the first sounds of Jim upstairs, he whimpered to the stairway door and lay down to wait, ready to spring into his usual explosive greeting. I was resigned to my fate as second potato.

And he still had just enough spunk to remain an all-around pain, getting his way at all costs. I caught him twice in our bed—upstairs!—when I got home from work. We had left the stairwell door closed! He must have learned all by himself to hurl his body against the door to bang it open. Obviously he wasn't scared of stairs enough to go up them. From then on we were forced to leave a chair reclined against the doorknob.

Eddie didn't like Jersey mail carriers any more than he did their California counterparts, scratching the front door each time the mail was delivered, so Jim also had to recline a chair against the knob of the front door. When people asked, I just pointed to the dog and said, "Home-styling by Eduardo."

I learned to appreciate the roomy house with a front porch and backyard and the pleasures of the suburbs—the humongous supermarkets, the uncrowded yoga studio, the quiet—and happily spent most of the week in the house. Jim left Bloomberg to return to Dow Jones, first to *SmartMoney* magazine, and after that magazine shut down its print edition, to *The Wall Street Journal*. Arielle and Henry were growing into young adulthood fast. Henry graduated with honors from his boarding school and started college. Arielle came to spend the summers with us and was able to get jobs in the city, becoming another Jersey commuter. Then she went to Ghana on her college year abroad and fell in love with the country. The next summer after that, after graduating, she headed back to Africa to work as an English teacher and later at an AIDS organization.

The only ones who still put up with Eddie in the bedroom were Henry and Arielle, letting him sleep with them when they visited. But Eddie was confused by the mixed messages. When visitors stayed over in the same guest room, he scratched the guest bedroom door, and if he was not let in, it was clack-clack-clack as he paced around, his paws on the hardwood floor making a deafening sound in the still of the night until the door opened. Our friend Clemson, a grade-school classmate of mine from Colegio San Antonio who was like a brother to me, let him in the first night he stayed with us, intending for Eddie to sleep at the foot of the bed. Five minutes later the dog was in bed with him. Thirty seconds later, Eddie was back out on his heinie. "I felt bad. He was alone and wanted company," Clemson told us the next morning as we made breakfast. "I went back to bed but for the next five minutes I just heard clack-clack-clack. But I didn't open the door."

Sometimes Eddie even tried his luck with Jim and me, scratching and rattling the stairway door after we said good night. Perhaps these two may let me sleep in their bed too? With no chair to block him, it sounded like he was throwing himself at the door. The first time he did it we tried to ignore him, but he was determined to keep us up all night on a work night. I felt Jim finally getting up.

"Don't go. Don't reward him with your attention," I said and turned over in bed. But Jim went. A few minutes later the door was shaking again.

"My turn," I told Jim. I got up and walked to the top of the stairs.

"Eddie, stop it!" I yelled. "Bad dog. Go to bed!"

That bought us a half hour.

When Jim's turn came again, he carried a rolled-up newspaper. We both had to get up early the next day and we were in no mood for let-me-in antics. At twelve fifty-four a.m. we all finally slept. A whack with the newspaper and Eddie finally got it, or so I thought. But the next morning I almost fell on my face as I tripped over Eddie's cushion, which Jim had moved to the hallway, "so he feels closer to us and less anxious," he explained.

"Something is up with him," said my husband as we all reassembled, bleary-eyed, in the dining room.

"I have no idea what it is, but he's unusually agitated and anxious.

The last time I went downstairs at night he was jumping out of his skin, dancing all over the place and panting heavily, like he had been chasing squirrels. I scheduled his annual checkup for this coming Saturday, so I'll ask the vet what he thinks. I wonder if it might relate in some way to his hearing loss and sounds he might be hearing in his head? Something is really spooking him."

Jim was up to his usual excuses, but I didn't mock him. I was too tired. Before he left on his bike, I heard Jim call Eddie "Bad dog!" by way of good-bye. Eddie looked suicidal, but even besotted owners have their limits.

"Hope you have a good day, darling," Jim e-mailed me later that morning. "Sorry again for the bad night but very nice to see your smile this morning. I don't know what got into your neurotic dog. XOXO."

Eddie just wanted what he wanted and he'd figure out a way to get it or make us pay. Peeing was still his favorite weapon, and he escalated the warfare in Montclair. On a night we came home from the theater late, I was getting water from the fridge when I heard Jim scream, "Bad dog!"

Jim was starting to sound like me. Now what?

"He peed in the freaking living room because he was mad at us for going out without him," Jim said as he ripped off half the roll of paper towel on the kitchen counter.

"Where?"

"Right smack square in the middle of the living room. You can't miss it."

"That is kind of passive-aggressive."

I walked to the closet to put away my coat with the indifference of someone who wouldn't be cleaning up the mess.

"What's so passive about it?" Jim said, irritated. He was looking in the utility closet for the bottle of Fantastik.

Ooooh, this was going to be good. Eddie was going to get his just deserts.

"What are you going to do, baby?"

"I'm going to tell him he's a very bad dog."

"And then you'll pet him?"

"No, I won't pet him."

"Or scratch him?"

"No, no scratching."

"Are you sure? Because that's giving him mixed messages."

"I'm going to whack him with a newspaper."

And he really did, but by then I had gone upstairs. It was late and I had already seen enough entertainment for the night.

"What did he do?" I asked Jim when he came to bed. "Did he look contrite?"

"He said if you don't want peeing in the living room, don't go out without me. If you don't like it, fix it."

"So what are you going to do about it?"

What he did was spread newspapers all over the living room. Always giving his dog the benefit of the doubt, Jim thought Eddie may have developed incontinence. Our living room, already covered with plastic, now looked like the inside of a dog crate. (And some friends still had the chutzpah to question why I kept my apartment in the city.)

One day, while putting on eye shadow, I noticed flakes and some bumpiness on my right eyelid. It didn't go away as the days passed, so I went to the dermatologist, who diagnosed some sort of eczema and tested me for fungus. The results came back positive.

"Do you have a dog?" she asked casually.

"I don't, but my husband sure does."

The doctor said it could have been passed on from the dog. Jim pet him and then pet me. He also sometimes picked me up at the train station with Eddie in the backseat of the car. Eddie always got all ruffled and would snort and try to get in the front seat as I got in, showering me with his bodily fluids. Eddie was literally making me sick. From then on, I made Jim wash his hands about twenty times a day.

Blame the dog, don't blame the dog, blame Jim—I didn't know how to feel other than fed up. I was still smarting from the medical news when we went over to Jim's boss's place on the Upper West Side for dinner. A former neighbor of Jim's from Fort Lauderdale, who also used to be friends with Jim's brother Arthur, was among the guests. Inevitably—I didn't know how it happened but it always did—the conversation turned to dogs and Eddie.

"What breed?" the boss asked.

Before I could catch myself, I blurted out: "A mix of heeler and asshole."

Shit. Now I had really done it. I was afraid to look at Jim. I really didn't mean to embarrass him in front of his editor. The words just flew out of my mouth. I concentrated on the halibut on my plate not daring to look up.

Then I heard Jim say: "Mostly asshole."

Everybody laughed.

I laughed the hardest.

A few days later, all laughing stopped. Eddie, so annoying, so conniving, so indestructible, looked like he was not going to make it.

Twelve

Epiphanies

E ddie wasn't looking so hot. I came home from work and found
Jim cooking a roasted chicken and potatoes with garlic brussels
sprouts for our Passover dinner. Uncharacteristically, Eddie was not
with him. I kissed Jim hello and headed for the closet to drop off my
coat. On my way, I saw Eddie slumped in his bed in the dining room,
glassy eyes open.

"What's wrong with Eddie?"

"He's been going downhill all afternoon," Jim said from the
kitchen. "He's been getting more lethargic. And this violent vomiting. He's vomited three or four times yellow bile."

Like the experienced father he was, Jim was worried, but not terribly so. He'd dealt with the occasional canine gastrointestinal problem and thought Eddie would snap out of it as usual. He'd throw up a few times, eat some grass, be okay.

But after our lovely Seder, just the two of us, Jim took Eddie out for a walk and noticed blood in his feces.

Jim looked a tad more worried when they came back. "He may have been poisoned."

I looked at Eddie and he was standing frozen in place, looking at us with a "This sucks" expression. He didn't seem to have the energy to move forward or to lie down. I had never seen him this listless. We tried to figure out what he could have possibly eaten. Could he have gotten poisoned from licking the grease at the bottom of the grill, a favorite forbidden pastime of his?

I didn't tell Jim, but I went upstairs to Google "dog poisoning." I was truly worried. Dead Eddie had never been part of my plan. I'd always wanted him to be far away but far away and alive, happily bugging someone else. Jim was supposed to leave early the next day for Florida for a week to work on his book with Dr. Marks, who headed south in the winter months. I wanted to make sure we knew what was going on before his plane took off.

The animal websites told me all I needed to know—vomiting, diarrhea, lethargy equaled an emergency. We needed to call the animal hospital.

I rushed downstairs and found Jim at the dining room table, watching over his ailing dog. Eddie was now lying on his cushion.

"Baby, I think you should take him to the hospital."

I summarized my findings. As usual, Jim took his time debating in his head the next step. He said that he didn't want to overreact. He thought it could pass and he was inclined to give Eddie the night to recover and see how he looked in the morning.

"When you have a dog, you don't want to take him in for every little problem," he said.

Yes, I knew, expensive, but I was actually terrified Jim would go on his trip and the mutt would die on me. Who would believe he died of natural causes under my watch?

"Baby, let's call the vet and see if you can postpone the trip. If Eddie gets sicker, you should be here when it happens. Don't take any chances."

Jim relented. He went online to look for a twenty-four-hour veterinary hospital close by. He found one in Fairfield, a town west of us less than half an hour away.

"I have a very sick dog," I heard Jim tell the hospital. "It appears he has some kind of bowel problem. He's passing blood. Can I bring him over right now?" Jim got some plastic bags and towels to put in the backseat of the car. It was almost midnight when he picked up his dog to carry him into the car.

At the hospital, blood tests and an examination showed that Eddie was severely dehydrated and at risk of kidney failure. His blood was like jam, really dense. They sedated him and put him on an IV to rehydrate him. It appeared there was some kind of major blockage in his bowels, but they didn't see an obvious cause. Jim came home close to two a.m., alone.

His face said it all.

"They said he needs to stay probably a couple of days at least. It doesn't look good."

We went to bed wondering if Eddie would last the night. Jim postponed the trip to Florida. We were on a deathwatch. Jim looked spent as we grappled with the possibility that Eddie would not get better.

"It's kind of like growing older, closing a chapter," he said. "Kind of saying farewell to a big, meaningful chunk of my life."

I couldn't sleep. I was reminded of my dear Mami—how a stupid, not even so serious fall in the bathroom set off a horrible chain of events and, within days, she was gone. And of my friend Dolores, who earlier in the year left the twentieth-anniversary party of my Latina group, Lips, saying she wasn't feeling well and who died the very same night after telling the paramedics, "I was at a party, dancing, for happiness." It was the dramatic exit of a playwright's last act as she succumbed to cardiac arrest.

"Where is that exit, exactly, and how do you sign up?" another Lipster, Michele, asked as we mourned.

Before the year was over, the Lipsters would lose another beloved "*hermana*," Elaine, a journalist and college professor who died of cirrhosis of the liver at fifty-four.

Here today, where tomorrow? I tossed and turned, thinking about mortality and about how Jim would take the death of his loyal companion of the last ten years. I knew Jim would have perspective on the death of his dog—"He's just a dog," as he often remarked himself— but there was no escaping the pain.

I imagined Jim telling the kids and their reaction. Arielle and Henry would be crushed. And me? I'd finally be released from a dog's annoyances, but I was not ready for no Eddie at all either. I was especially not ready for the guilt, which kicked in abruptly.

Eddie had been a fixture in the household, always there when we came home. The relentless companion—even in the bathroom— who wouldn't take no for an answer. He had been the topic of conversation, the icebreaker, the safe subject when the rest of our stepfamily had been too mad or too distant to talk about anything else at the dinner table. He no longer drew our attention by squirming to scratch his back on the carpet like he used to in the Palisades—because we had no carpet in Montclair—but he still snored through dinner in his corner of the dining room or got up five times to sneak under the table. He was so adept that we wouldn't notice until one of us crossed our legs and bumped into him or felt a slight brush as he scrounged around our laps for crumbs.

We had all shared his dog-walking adventures, the same disgust when he smelled, even though the farting was not always his fault no matter what the other males in the house might have you believe. He'd been the one common denominator that everyone loved. Yes, even me. It is not true that he had given me no pleasure, I realized now. I had reached for the leash every time I needed to take a deep breath. "Come on, Eddie. Let's walk." Eddie had been a calming companion, my therapy dog. He'd offered me temporary allegiance. He'd revealed to me the innocence behind a teenager's sullen front. He'd helped me get to know my husband better and exposed his tender side. How could I not love my husband more when Eddie barked and Jim thanked him for protecting us? Eddie had been a unifier. He had connected us.

And what was Eddie's big sin, after all? Loving my husband. Guarding him against threats, real and imagined. Being his friend—needy as hell, yes, but loyal.

Shit.

After the battles that raged on for years between us, the mutt was playing his last card to win.

"He was in great pain," Jim said as we lay in bed. He couldn't sleep either. "He was really unhappy. He just had a very melancholy look on his face. He was passing blood. He knew he was sick. He felt awful. I felt terrible for him. He was so stricken."

I knew what Jim was thinking. If Eddie had to go, he—we—hoped it would be fast.

We had friends who had gone through hell with their sick dogs. My friend Tammy went through a long ordeal with her dog Sophie, who deteriorated slowly until she stopped walking altogether. At first, Tammy treated Sophie's arthritis with expensive meds. She also took her to acupuncture appointments every month. She bought a ramp to help the dog get up and down the three steps to the den.

"People make comments because of how funny she walks," Tammy said during one of her calls from Oakland, California, where she lived in a house not far from a lake with a footpath popular with joggers and dog walkers.

Sophie, a fifty-eight-pound boxer–pit bull–beagle mix, suffered from severe separation anxiety that didn't lessen as she grew more infirm. She would start hyperventilating and howling if she saw Tammy leaving. But now Sophie could barely walk.

"She likes to go places, but a lot of places I can't take her because I have to carry her," Tammy said. "The other day I threw out my back."

Tammy bought straps to lift the dog up from under the stomach, but Sophie was too heavy. She also got pieces of rug that she tossed around the house. She was hoping they would give Sophie some traction on the tile floors so she would be able to stand up. Nothing was effective in getting Sophie moving.

The vet told Tammy, "You know what's going to happen, right?"

"No, what?"

"It's going to get hard to clean up after her and that's going to be the time to put her to sleep."

But Tammy wouldn't hear of it.

"She's like an old person," Tammy said.

And Sophie still enjoyed going out. Tammy was not about to spend seven hundred dollars on a wheelchair with four wheels, so she got her a little wagon for eighty dollars at Target. She got Sophie a blanket and off they'd go for a roll around Lake Merritt.

But one day Sophie couldn't get up. She could only relieve herself lying down on her side. Tammy got her a big pee pad. She and her mom took the dog to a canine orthopedic specialist, after waiting three weeks for an appointment.

"They were jam-booked with other crazy parents," Tammy told me.

During the consultation, the specialist produced a big rubber ball. Tammy was instructed to balance Sophie on the ball—with her stomach over the ball and legs on the ground—and bounce her up and down to exercise her legs. Tammy bought the ball. But Sophie hated it and refused to cooperate. The ball went to the junk heap.

"If they don't think she's a candidate for hydrotherapy or something else that could get her up on her feet, at least able to go to the bathroom and walk a little, I'm going to have to put her to sleep pretty soon," Tammy said, and I could feel her dread over the line.

"At least she doesn't seem to be in any pain. There's certainly nothing wrong with her nose or appetite, which is good."

Despite all efforts, Sophie became completely incontinent and started to whine pitifully. The day before Labor Day weekend, Tammy took her to the vet and said good-bye to her friend.

"It was basically a progressive descent into hell," Tammy said much later. "If there is one lesson I learned, it's that you should put them to sleep before it gets to that foul point."

"Sounds nuts as I look at it in retrospect."

Sophie was thirteen, Eddie's contemporary.

But Eddie survived the night.

When Jim went back in the morning to see him, they told him they wanted to keep the dog on the IV. They urged him not to see him. He'd get too excited, too agitated. Eddie stayed one more night and day before Jim took him to his regular vet, Dr. Cameron, closer to us, on Bloomfield Avenue. Dr. Cameron wanted to keep Eddie for observation. Eddie stayed, getting nutrients and antibiotics, another four nights.

"How's Eddie, honey?" I asked Jim on the phone from work after he'd had his daily morning chat with the vet.

"Better. The vet may let him come home."

They never learned why exactly his bowels were blocked. That would have required surgery. It could have been that he ate something awful and got an infection. A few months earlier Jim had gotten him leather bones to chew on. It could have been that. Eddie wasn't supposed to eat them, but he gobbled them down. We were now supposed to feed him only some medicinal canned food the doctor ordered, some prescription diet for canine gastrointestinal health. After a week, we could start feeding him with a mixture of dry and regular canned food. Jim said the dry food was not sitting well with Eddie and he was getting diarrhea periodically.

"I'll help you nurse him back to health, baby."

Yes. I would make it up to the mutt. I hadn't been too horrible to him, right? In my defense, there were worse dog owners than I am. We had a friend who was much more disdainful of the family dog, a cute little thing named Lola. He got steamrolled by his wife and kids and ended up with a poodle mix he refused to look after in any way and called "Stupid." I knew of another case where the wife made the husband give up the dog. I never gave Jim an it's-me-or-the-dog ultimatum. (Wonder what Jim . . . Nah.) My conscience, for the most part, was clear.

But Eddie and I had to try harder. Our hate-hate relationship needed to evolve into at least love-hate.

Eddie came home from the hospital a bit thinner, but like his old self—all tongue and spots and hysterical tail. He immediately went to his bed in the dining room, positioned himself head down and butt aloft, waiting for Jim and their scratching ritual.

"There you are, there you go," Jim said as he complied. "I missed you too, buddy."

I looked on, genuinely sharing in the joy.

Eddie was elated to be home, running back and forth from room to room.

When he stopped wheezing past me, I bent down and pet him. "Hello, Eddie. Did you miss me too?"

I decided I'd pet him more and not hold any more grudges. I'd be a more involved stepmom.

He lingered a few seconds longer than usual under my touch. He'd missed me too.

I watched Jim give Eddie his antibiotic pills with peanut butter, feeding them by hand, and I found myself feeling the happiness of the moment. Eddie almost bit Jim's hand off at the first taste of the unexpected treat.

"Ouch, you're biting me. Ouch, ouch, ouch." Jim faked great pain as Eddie licked the last bit of peanut butter from his fingers. What a pair those two were.

A couple of months after Eddie's bout with near death, I ran into

Jim's colleague Elizabeth on the train to Montclair. Her dog had died recently and she talked about the terrible feeling of emptiness. She said she had a harder time dealing with the dog's passing than when her kids left home to go to college.

"She was always there," she said. "She was the definition of home."

For a moment I tried to imagine life without Eddie and I couldn't. He was the definition of our home too.

Elizabeth's dog died at sixteen and was healthy up to the last two years or so, when she went blind and senile. "I'd say let's go! And she'd just look at me," Elizabeth said.

I made a mental note: to watch for Eddie not recognizing the word "walk" as the beginning of the end.

Thirteen

Mia and Eddie—A Love Story After All?

In yoga class one night, on a full moon, Kerri, our teacher, asked us to write down the emotions we wanted to be released from. I wrote down "selfishness."

Eddie's near-death experience gave me fuzzy feelings that were not reciprocated. In no time he went back to what he did best. Scratch-scratch-bang-bang on the stairwell door at one in the morning. Piss-piss-piss behind the sofa in the living room despite his numerous walks. Woof-woof-woof at me, whenever he felt like it.

The doors showed deep creases and the living room sometimes smelled like the corners of a subway station.

"I don't know," Jim said, defeated, after one restless night when we took turns yelling at the dog from the top of the stairs to stop the incessant scratching. "He's a cranky old fart."

Still, I needed to make it up to this cranky old fart. In our competitive relationship, it was no longer all about my feelings.

For the first time, I wanted to do something I never cared for before. I was going to try to understand this dog. His aging had softened me up enough to care about what was in his head. Maybe empathy would be less stressful. I wanted to learn about the psyche of dogs. What motivated them other than food, walks, and finding a soft surface for snoring? How could they be so lovable yet so stupid? How did you win them over?

Of course, there was no shortage of material. A cursory check on Amazon produced *The Dog's Mind, Inside of a Dog, Think Dog!, Dog Psychology, You Are a Dog, Why Do Dogs Drink Out of the Toilet?*, and so on. I ordered the least deranged-sounding titles and, I had to admit, I was fascinated by some of what I read. Dogs, as most people into dogs already know, evolved from wolves centuries ago. They became domesticated after they began hanging out with humans. Soon tired of their pets' wolfish appearance, the humans began breeding them into many shapes and looks, until they finally got Trouble, the cute Maltese that inherited twelve million dollars from hotel chain empress Leona Helmsley. (A judge thought that was crazy and later reduced the inheritance down to two million dollars.) As I read on, some of Eddie's nutty behavior started to make sense. He sometimes kicked dirt after relieving himself because he wanted the odor to waft farther away, signaling to other dogs that he was the man. The importance of smell to a dog explained almost everything, in fact. It was why they made a beeline for crotches and one another's rumps.

Some things, like the appetite for other dogs' feces, were still a mystery, though. Even the ASPCA was flummoxed. "There is no apparent reason for this strange behavior," its website said.

And dogs could bark for all sorts of reasons—as a greeting or to get attention—not necessarily hostility, I learned. But I knew my Eddie. Could he have just been saying "Hello!" all these years? Nah. It was more like "Scram!," "Don't touch him!," "Take that!," "And that!," "I'm going to bite you any minute now!" He tried to intimidate me. He wanted me gone.

How could I stop the hate? A Lipster, Rose, referred me to a friend who worked at the San Francisco Society for the Protection of Animals. She in turn referred me to Jeannine Berger, the director of behavior resources at the San Francisco SPCA's Veterinary Hospital. She's a DVM and DACVB, which I had to look up. A doctor of veterinary medicine and a diplomate, or board-certified specialist, of the American College of Veterinary Behaviorists. A pet shrink! After couples therapy, could I now be entertaining the notion of going to therapy with my husband's dog? What the heck. Nothing to lose but my dignity.

I e-mailed her, asking if we could talk about the issues that may arise when someone fell in love with a dog owner and the dog acted like Glenn Close in *Fatal Attraction*.

The good doctor wrote back:

"Dear Mia. Many of my clients experience similar feelings like you. The issues are usually not 'dog wars'—they are 'people wars' and the dogs are the innocent casualties that suffer from the inconsistency in the home."

All aboard! As if I could ever doubt whose side she was going to take.

But I tried not to be defensive. I put on my reporter's cap and called the expert. Dr. Berger told me she commonly heard from couples and roommates complaining that the dog had become a source of conflict in the household, much like housekeeping chores or loud snoring. She set me straight about the term "jealous dogs." That was an anthropomorphism, she said, meaning I was attributing human characteristics to an animal.

"Jealousy is usually how the other human feels, the one that does not have that close relationship with the dog," she said.

Bah.

If a dog was very close to one person in the home and disliked others in the family, she explained, then usually one of two things was going on. One, the dog was fearful of that person, or two, the dog considered the person a competitor for a resource, in this case our shared man. Either way, she said, the problem was fairly easy to address in most cases. She suggested I look up an animal behaviorist in my area to assess Eddie's needs and devise a treatment plan "from the dog's point of view."

Right, like I was about to bring another Eddie ally into our home.

"From Eddie's point of view, all that needs to happen is for me to disappear," I joked.

Dr. Berger calmly explained that dogs make a strong connection to one family member, they feel an affiliation "like a child or a person would." Hostility happened frequently. A couple got a dog and the dog bonded with one person. The other person might trigger fear. It was up to this person to alleviate the fear or make it worse.

That was me.

I came in after Eddie, an unfamiliar human in the household. And in his beady eyes, apparently, I became a competitor for resources like attention and love. To turn things around, I could start by becoming a "provider" of resources, Dr. Berger suggested.

"You just have to find out what's high-value for Eddie."

That was easy. Food. What else? We're talking a dog that once rose on his hind legs to reach a box of fund-raising chocolate bars on the kitchen counter and ate all ten bars. He pooped aluminum foil for days. I could become the "food dispenser," Dr. Berger suggested. And I could make more of an impression, she said, if I bestowed enticing treats like cheese, chicken, or Cheerios.

That'd work, I agreed. Eddie would definitely reconsider his animosity if I surprised him with a tasty morsel. I had one concern, though. Eddie followed many of my orders more or less without treats, even if he forgot two minutes later. He still obeyed me, eventually, after he feigned a limp or deafness. Exposed to a system of rewards, would he become an even bigger pain in the ass? And if I stop feeding him, would he go back to his old ways? "Do I have to reward him all the time?"

"Would you work for no pay?" Dr. Berger replied.

Well, no, but I loved for no pay. Whatever happened to the dog was like a child? Weren't dogs supposed to offer unconditional love like their smitten owners kept saying? Weren't they innocent, selfless teachers? You couldn't have it both ways. Either dogs were like innocent children or they were shameless extortionists.

But I kept quiet. At this point, I just wanted a permanent truce.

I was skeptical that a geezer like Eddie could still learn new tricks. Dr. Berger said an old dog could indeed change. As if in passing, she mentioned that she often found that the real problem was usually not the dog but the couple's relationship. She had seen many examples of this. Dig a little deeper, she said, and soon you'd find something else gnawing at the partners.

"Do couples ever break up over the dog?" I asked, a bit taken aback.

"I wouldn't know, but I've seen couples come in and fight over the dog and you know that the dog is not the real issue."

I hung up with my throat constricting. This harmless fact-finding mission had backed me into a corner. No more denial. We were, of course, one of those couples. We just found it much easier to ignore the real tension in the marriage and deal with the sporadic fight without ever solving anything. But true happiness had eluded us because it came down to this: I loved Jim deeply, and he loved me, but we had failed at negotiating my place in the family. He still felt a conflict between his role as father and that of husband. I'd yet to fit his children into my life. Even now that the kids were adults, there was a code of silence. We talked about them peripherally, avoiding the land mines. When they visited, we were all automatically transported back to the Palisades. They inhabited their world with Jim, and I inhabited mine. We had suffered the fate of many stepfamilies—alienation, cordial relations at best. It had been our collective loss. Eddie's hostility, or even worse, his indifference, was a constant reminder of what didn't work in my blended family. Eddie had been an easy scapegoat, my voodoo doll. The kids were untouchable, the husband unwavering, but I could go on and on *about the dog*.

It had taken a pet shrink to face the truth and make me want to do something about it. I so wished to embrace stepmotherhood. I spoke to Jim's kids infrequently now that we were apart. I knew about their lives mostly as relayed by their father. But if I could reinvent my relationship with the dog, could the kids be next? I was not sure if building substantial relationships with my adult stepchildren would ever be possible. Even if we all wanted to give it a shot, distance was an issue now. Henry lived with his mother in California while working and going to college. Arielle was working abroad. But Eddie was still here. I could at least give him a break. There was no denying that the dog was an inescapable relationship within my family. He was my stepdog. I could still be a good stepmother. I would strive to end a ten-year conflict.

Yes, I would become the food dispenser!

Jim immediately nixed the idea of giving Eddie human food.

"People have the crazy idea that if you feed human food to dogs that you're doing them a favor, that it's making them part of the family, and from everything I know, it's terrible for dogs," he told me. "Eddie, his stomach gets screwed up. It's way too rich for him and he gets diarrhea."

Thank you, Dr. Sterngold. I didn't know Jim was so passionate about what went into Eddie's mouth. I reminded myself we almost lost him to poisoning.

"Sometimes he'll find crap on the ground and, if he manages to wolf down a piece of a sandwich or pizza, more often than not he'll get diarrhea," Jim went on. "I'm not going to clean up the diarrhea."

Me neither.

I really didn't feel that strongly about it. I was okay with bribing Eddie with dog treats instead. I was eager to start, but the food dispensing needed to be postponed until Jim and I returned from a long-planned trip to Vietnam. It would be an unusually long kennel stay for our senior doggie—twelve days. But the kennel loved him and had become his second home.

A few days later, Jim and I bobbed in the waters of spectacular Ha Long Bay on a junk. We found Vietnam surprisingly welcoming of Americans—they were more preoccupied with China now—and well recovered physically from the war. Vital signs like a market economy and a population that skewed young were clearly healthy. We made long visits to the war museum in Saigon and the perplexing Cu Chi tunnels where the Vietcong hid and showed steely determination. Jim and I fired a gun for the first time in an open-air shooting gallery where visitors could pick the war weapon of their choice. We chose the M16 used by American soldiers and became even more anti-gun.

In Hanoi, we came across a board sign outside a café.

"Doggie-style tour," it read. "Includes dog meat and local dishes. Beer and rice wine. Sunset over West Lake."

American dogs. When they were overweight, their owners sent them to the gym. Their Vietnamese brethren on the other side of the world were instead skinned, seasoned, and served to anyone willing to cough up a few dong. (Dogs supposedly were good for virility and warmth in the winter months; cats were spared because they eat rats.)

"I wonder how Eddie is," I mentioned to Jim one night over a dinner.

"Plotting his revenge," Jim said. "'I'm going to shit on his bed, and then I'm going to piss on his sofa.'"

But when we got back from our trip, Eddie was as meek as could be, back to his clingy, whimpery self after a face-saving period of indifference to punish Jim. As usual, he looked at me with a you're-still-here look of resignation and behaved as if it were such a chore to be around me.

But Edweirdo was in for a surprise. He'd have to rely on me from now on for his sustenance. His routine was to be fed twice a day, after his morning and evening walks. The delicious menu consisted of Science Diet's ground "gourmet chicken (or beef) entrée" and Eukanuba's "maintenance" formula, dry pellets that had the added benefit of also reducing tartar and plaque buildup (but, apparently, not bad breath). Eddie liked the wet food much better, so he was prone to eat around the pellets and leave the dry food on the dish. He didn't eat the dry food unless he was bored as a clam—usually after he'd licked his paws, taken a nap, scratched himself behind the ears, paced around the house sniffing corners, and banged against closed doors. As the new food dispenser, I was determined to mash the two kinds of food so thoroughly that he had to eat it all. On the first day of my new job, a Sunday, I slept in. By the time I made it to the kitchen shortly before ten a.m., Jim was more anxious than the dog.

"He's jumping out of his skin waiting for his breakfast," he announced.

I looked at Eddie, sprawled on the floor looking at us, and he seemed all right. In fact, he had gotten up to let me pet him by way of greeting—no growling—so he was better than all right. You never knew with his moods.

I took a cupful of his dry food and mixed it with a half can of wet food, smashing the dry pellets into the soft glob. I placed the bowl down and he almost bit my fingers off to get to it. Yum-yum. He loved his food. He inhaled it. Soon I saw the effect of my effort. I was upstairs, reading in the bedroom, while Jim was out running errands, when I heard Eddie whimpering outside the bedroom door. What? The mutt has breached the off-limits area again!

"Eddie!" I screamed.

He knew he'd been a bad dog and headed back for the stairs, but, again, the poor thing was scared to go down the steps. He didn't think ahead as usual. I prodded him gently, holding his collar, so he was reassured he wouldn't tumble down. As we stepped down I wondered—could this breach be a sign of new affection?

Sure thing! Between the second and third food-dispensing weeks most barking at me stopped as if we had turned off a switch.

What a feeling of accomplishment that first bark-free morning. I came down the stairs and Eddie was in his usual spot in the kitchen, behind his boyfriend's legs. Now that he didn't hear so well he sometimes didn't sense me until I was right next to him. As I leaned in to kiss Jim, Eddie began to grunt but caught himself, as if he just remembered that I served breakfast. He looked away sheepishly and pretended he had found something interesting to sniff on the floor.

The next morning, I came down to the dining room and he didn't leap to bark at me as I passed his inert body. He was in his bed, his eyes were wide open, but I heard nary a peep as I leaned in to kiss Jim. This was awesome. How ignorant we had been. People should all go to doggie school before they are allowed to own a dog. It'd avert so much misery.

"There's nothing in between—either he's in love with you and he can't live a moment without you," Jim said with a chuckle, "or he's going to eat your face off if you fall asleep."

A loving Eddie, of course, brought its own irritations. For one thing, this new appreciation for his stepmom didn't seem genuine. I fed him and all of a sudden he found me acceptable? But my worries were for naught because Jim began sabotaging my food dispensing soon into the new routine.

"I fed Eddie," he chirped from the dining room as I entered the kitchen to make my morning coffee a few days later.

"Why?"

"Sorry, it's my routine. I forget sometimes."

"I forget" were fighting words. They instantly put me in a bad mood. They took me back to the Palisades years when I was always out of the loop, when he'd ask me to help one of the kids with homework and then sit within earshot "reading" a book, as if to say: "I'm here nearby, don't worry, in case stepmom attacks." It felt then like he was sabotaging my efforts to bond. Now he was doing it again.

Was it possible Jim purposely didn't want to let go of Eddie, even this little allowance? I'd also noticed he always found something to do in the kitchen—make a snack, empty out the dishwasher—while I prepared Eddie's meal. Maybe I was suffering from post-traumatic stress syndrome.

"You are undermining me," I told him. "It's a pattern."

Jim laughed it off. "Now you think you're the dog Freud," he said. But he did it again, always ready with an excuse for feeding Eddie.

"I didn't want to wake you and he seemed uncomfortable."

Or: "He's gotten into this thing where he scratches the floor. He was driving me crazy."

When I approached Jim one morning, Eddie growled and barked. It was the first time he returned to his old habit since I started feeding him.

"No!" Jim commanded. "You're not going to start that again. You're a new dog."

Eddie waited for a pat, but there was no petting or mercy this time from Jim, who knew I was pissed.

"Stop sabotaging me," I warned him. "If we're not going to do it well, I shouldn't bother."

"You should bother. I'll do my best."

"Don't do your best. Just do it."

"I'm with you one hundred percent."

Jim fulfilled his promise. He stopped feeding Eddie and started nagging me.

"Eddie needs his breakfast!"

That was my husband's new "Good morning" for a few days, until we found our food-dispensing groove.

Ultimately, Eddie remained hot and cold with me, which was better than mostly cold. One evening, as I was watching TV in the den, he came over and sat quietly in front of me. He didn't have the psycho look he got when he was desperate for a walk. And he wasn't giving me his back like he did when he was ready to race me to Jim. It took me a few seconds to realize what was going on. He was waiting for his dinner! I was taken aback by how good it felt to have him sitting there needing me. Now I got it. This was what Jim cherished the most and maybe had been afraid to lose, to let go of—feeling needed. Oy. I was brimming with dog-fueled insights, but it wasn't all good. I had to work hard to let go of new waves of resentment, of the shoulda, woulda, coulda. What was done was done.

I would find a way to assuage Jim's fears, if in fact he harbored them, and to make him understand I stood no chance to replace him with the dog or kids because that had never been my intention.

Fall came, the days were cooler, and Eddie underwent his seasonal personality change, from lethargic to perky. All of a sudden he had more energy, wagged his tail faster, foraged for food in all corners of the house with more conviction, whimpered louder, scratched doors more forcefully, slept less, and followed us more. He was back to his healthy self and for the first time I felt I had played a role in his nurturing and recovery. I cared about him.

It felt good, even if the fireworks were still reserved for Jim.

The news from the vet after his latest checkup was not good, though.

"Darling, Eddie may be sick. He may be seriously sick," Jim said as the two of them got back from the doctor's office.

"What? What's wrong?"

"So I took Eddie to Dr. Cameron and everything is fine. He weighs forty-two pounds. Squirmed like crazy. Hated being there. All the normal healthy stuff. But Dr. Cameron listened to his heart and immediately said, 'Has he had a heart murmur before?' I said, 'No, not to my knowledge.' And he said, 'Well, he has a really bad one. It's a three over six,' whatever that means. That's how they measure it, I guess. He said, 'This is really a bad sign if I didn't hear anything a year ago. And now it's three over six. It's been incremental at a very fast pace. You need to see a cardiologist right away and get a sonogram and get a definitive diagnosis of exactly what it is that's wrong.'"

Jesus. This was unexpected, because there had been no symptoms of anything.

"Is it life-threatening?" I asked Jim.

He didn't answer.

I hugged my husband. "Baby, you take such good care of Eddie." I tried a joke: "So no more vodka for Eddie?"

"No more martinis for Eddie," Jim said, lightening up a bit. "He'll miss the olives."

On the day of his ten a.m. appointment with the cardiologist, a fasting Eddie was vacuuming under the refrigerator and the cabinets while Jim ate his breakfast. The two left in Jim's brand-new Prius, the fuel-efficient hybrid electric car that replaced our old station wagon. Eddie loved the Prius. It brought him one seat closer to Jim, allowing him to pant in his ear during rides and get a scratch or two at stoplights.

Not long after they left, Jim called on his way back from the doctor. "Things are okay. Your mutt is going to make it. We paid six hundred dollars for the doctor to say bring him back if he gets sick."

That old geezer. He was indestructible. That night over dinner, Jim and I joked we should put him in our respective wills. You never knew.

"Really, Jim, he may outlive us."

"I'd have to think who could take him."

Henry and Arielle were the obvious candidates, but between work and college they were not immediately available. We really had no one else, so we shelved the subject and toasted to our good health instead.

The Saturday of Martin Luther King Day weekend, Jim and I planned a party. We called it Octavitas, in keeping with the Puerto Rican tradition of stretching the Christmas and Three Kings' Day holiday for eight extra days. Our tree was still up and we partied Puerto Rican–style—drinking *coquito*, eating *pasteles*, turkey, and ham, and dancing salsa and merengue until early morning. Jim and I were so happy about the turnout of close to thirty friends that we decided to host Octavitas parties every January.

The next morning, the birds chirped, the dog sniffed, and Jim and I sipped our strong coffee at the dining table while partaking of that old American custom known as holding a newspaper. Jim made waffles for me and our friend Clemson, who had stayed over. We lingered around the breakfast table, happily gossiping about the party and skimming the Sunday *Times*. Before me was a day of lazy chores—cleaning out my office topped the list—and I left the table first. A couple of hours later, Jim swung by my office all layered up for riding in thirty-five-degree weather.

Jim had taken up biking for exercise a few months earlier. He could no longer run with his worn-out knees. He'd been getting painful shots of a lubricant for his knees once a week. But he had taken to biking like a little kid. Clemson, an experienced rider, had been coaching him and giving him expensive hand-me-downs. Jim now showed up in my office in full multicolor bike gear and posed sideways all proud of himself. For this ride, he was wearing bib shorts with straps that looked like suspenders and made him look like a Ukrainian wrestler. He also put on long biking pants and a multicolored jersey cluttered with brand names—Subaru, Shimano, Dell, LeMond, Gary Fisher, Harman Kardon—in red, yellow, blue, and black. He looked fit and healthy and Tour de France athletic for a ride on the busy streets of Montclair.

I almost told him to be careful and not overdo it showing off to Clemson—men—but I stopped myself. I had been nagging him lately about the dangers of bicycling but he didn't want to hear it. He was the man.

"The turkey gumbo is simmering on the stove," he said on his way out.

The plan was for them to come back, watch football all afternoon, and eat the gumbo, made with the turkey bone leftovers from the party. Jim was going to serve it over white rice and I planned to make plantain *tostones*, my specialty.

The phone rang not even fifteen minutes after Jim and Clemson left for their bike ride.

It was Clemson.

"I have some bad news."

Fourteen

Third Wheel

What?" I said, trying not to think.

"Jim had an accident and the ambulance is going to take him to . . . what's the hospital's name? . . . Universal Hospital. Hold on, here's the paramedic."

I waited on the phone, holding my breath and thinking that I knew all along something like this would happen. I viewed bikes as I do motorcycles—not worth the risk. Yet, scores of my colleagues and friends rode those stupid Citi Bikes all over New York, sharing the road with aggressive drivers of cars, cabs, and buses and ignoring the frequency with which those cars, cabs, and buses ran over bikers and pedestrians. Clemson, who lived an hour north in Garrison and who rode on country roads, was himself hit by a car in Bear

Mountain State Park not long ago. Inside a park! But he still got Jim all enthused about biking and there he was, on a lazy Sunday, riding behind my husband when somehow Jim did a flip and landed on his face. Damn you, Clemson.

"He has a concussion, but he is conscious," the paramedic said on the phone. "Is he allergic to any medication?"

Was my husband allergic to any medication? He hardly ever got sick.

"No."

I rushed to get dressed, trying not to panic, but my thoughts were hitting the alarm button. Clemson didn't want to tell me the truth over the phone, that's why he gave the phone to the medic. Jim was paralyzed. Jim would be dead by the time I got to the hospital. I thought about how I jumped out of bed that morning when he wanted me to linger, about what a bitch I'd been to begrudge him spoiling his children and his dog, about wanting to get rid of Eddie when he was already facing an empty nest, about a thousand more regrets. I'd accused Jim of wearing rose-colored glasses, but I had benefited from his positive outlook, from his good nature, from his looking past my flaws. I had been a control freak, hardheaded. Pretending not to be vulnerable didn't make me any less so, it was obvious now. I had a partner who loved me. It wasn't just me, alone in the world. I loved and was loved. Was this how you lost your husband? I didn't want to be a widow. I'd go right after him, I didn't care.

As thoughts attacked from all directions, I cursed Clemson, again, because he was blocking our car with his car in the driveway and because there I was looking online and there was no such thing as Universal Hospital in New Jersey. There was, however, a University Hospital in Newark that was part of Rutgers University. While

I waited for Clemson to get back, I got a change of clothes for Jim and looked in his file cabinet for medical insurance records. He was so organized that I found the information quickly. When I couldn't sit anymore, I put Eddie on the leash and took him out for a walk. Innocent, naive, unsuspecting Eddie. If he only knew. I watched him trot along and thought of his devotion to Jim. Eddie would be my only comfort if the worst were to happen. I knew so because, after 9/11, I interviewed widows with arms wrapped around their husbands' dogs as they spoke of their tragedy. Eddie and I would be inseparable, united in mourning for the same love. Wasn't that something? Jim would not have believed it.

Half an hour went by before Clemson showed up on his bike, followed by a patrol car with Jim's bike in the trunk. I asked the officer where the hell they had taken my husband. University Hospital in Newark. On the way to the hospital, Clemson told me what had happened.

"We were on a flat stretch of Ridgewood Avenue, approaching Bay Avenue. We were cruising at eighteen to twenty miles per hour and I was watching his form and technique and, all of sudden, his rear wheel goes up and he goes upside down and hits the ground hard. He's knocked out. No screaming or 'Whoa!' He did a cartwheel, went up and over, and came down hard on head and face, and he was knocked out with his eyes open."

I listened and drove, trying hard to keep it together and not go back to my worst-case-scenario trance. Jim was knocked out for a few minutes but his eyes had remained open, Clemson said. What did that mean? As he was calling 911, Clemson said, he had checked Jim's breathing and mouth to make sure he was not swallowing his tongue. Jim was bleeding on the right side from an opened eyebrow. They were fortunate that two cars stopped immediately—one with a father and son and the other one with a couple. She was a nurse and squatted by Jim to take his vital signs and keep him still.

"I think he's going to be okay," she told Clemson as two cop cars arrived and she deferred to the officers.

Jim made some noises and moved his legs, Clemson said. But he wasn't responding to questions. He tried to get up and Clemson had to tackle his legs to prevent him from moving. The paramedics arrived and took over. They put him on a board and spent fifteen minutes deciding where to go. There was Mountainside Hospital nearby in Montclair, but they took him to the bigger hospital with the trauma center twenty minutes away.

We got to the hospital and when I saw Jim laid up in his emergency room cubicle, I almost fainted from all the blood—on his face, his clothes, the gauzes strewn about on the floor. The right side of his face looked like a butcher's cut, his eye lost in skin. He was a swollen, misshapen mess, but he was alert. I tried to focus my gaze on the one limpid blue eye that was open and tearing up looking at me. I squeezed his hand and cried along.

"I'm here, baby."

My poor baby. I felt so immensely sad for him. He had been so happy and healthy only hours before, only to end up like this, on a hospital bed looking like a character from a Quentin Tarantino movie. Aside from the eye swollen shut, he was dark purple from lid to cheek on his right side. Streaks of blood ran down the cheek to his neck. Half his face was raw from road rash. His upper lip was also swollen and purple. He was wearing a neck brace. I didn't know where to begin.

"What's wrong with his neck?" I asked one of the resident doctors hovering over him.

"Just a precaution until the results of X-rays are back."

"I don't remember what happened," Jim kept repeating. He looked disoriented, so childlike and defenseless, I just wanted to bring him to my bosom and hold him. Four resident doctors worked around us, ready to stitch him up. They were very young and seemed impressed with the bike injury.

"What kind of bike do you ride?" one of them asked Jim.

"A Cannondale road bike," Jim answered weakly.

Good. He didn't say President Barack Obama. And good that the doctors were relating on a personal level. They might not kill him. I spotted a plastic bag with Jim's helmet and clothes by a wall. All the expensive attire had been cut off of him. I looked through swaths of fabric from what used to be the bib shorts and jersey and the checkered red vest his mom had given him ages ago. The helmet was also in the bag, badly scuffed and stained with blood. Without a doubt, it protected him. The shoes had made it intact, just like his teeth.

The doctors asked me to take a chair outside the curtain while they stitched up his eyebrow and eyelid—fourteen stitches across the brow, another ten across the lid and temple. We then waited for the results of a CT scan. Clemson was outside in the general waiting room, doing penance. Poor Clemson. He was shaken up by the accident too. He was a kind friend. I got over my anger.

An hour went by and as I sat watching the goings-on in the emergency room it became evident why the paramedics decided to take Jim to Newark. The ER was busier than Penn Station. It dealt with all kinds of mayhem. In quick succession, I saw patients wheeled in and out with open wounds and broken bones. A twentysomething woman glided by on a stretcher with her neck in a cast, her purse and shopping bags tucked safely by her legs. A group of cops and paramedics wheeled in an older guy with blood trickling from his left eye. He'd been punched in the head and kicked in the chest while walking on Seventh Street, a robbery victim in plain daylight on a Sunday afternoon.

"Did you lose consciousness?" a doctor asked from behind his curtain.

"How many guys?" the cops wanted to know.

The victim, who said he was sixty-seven, was lucid and answered every question.

"Go get them, Officer," a jovial nurse told the cops on their way out.

"There are, like, a million of them," replied a female officer as she walked out writing on a pad.

Moments later, another man came in on a stretcher trailed by escorts. A prisoner. I couldn't hear what was wrong with him, but two officers stood guard outside his curtain for the rest of the evening. Between perp and victim, there lay my beloved. With his grade-one concussion (mild), no bleeding in the brain, and no broken bones, it turned out that Jim was in relatively good shape. I asked the resident doctor who told us Jim could go home, a Dr. Chandler, how soon my husband could go to work. I knew Jim would want to wait all of two or three days before trying to resume normal activities and I was hoping the doctor would dissuade him.

"What does he do?"

"He's a journalist."

"Oh, yeah? Where?"

"Wall Street Journal."

Dr. Benjamin Chandler happened to be the son of a former editor of the *New York Post*, Ken Chandler.

"So how come you didn't follow in his footsteps," I asked him as we chitchatted about the coincidence.

"He worked crazy hours," he said.

An emergency room doctor thinks journalists work crazy hours? Jim and I laughed.

I brought Clemson in after Jim was stitched up to describe the fall to the doctors. Now he and I tried to get Jim to get up, but he couldn't. He complained about terrible back and shoulder pain on his right side. A cycling friend of Clemson's, a nurse, kept texting him that it'd be prudent to keep Jim in the hospital for observation. The ER docs ultimately decided to keep him overnight. He was transferred to a hospital room, where the nurses tucked him in and I fed him some yogurt bought from a cafeteria snack machine. Jim was chatty and very much sounding like himself again. Clemson and I left after midnight. Clemson, a Spanish-language sports announcer, had a Knicks game the next day, the MLK holiday, so I went back to the hospital alone the next morning to retrieve my husband.

I found Jim sitting in a chair, smiling, with his black-and-purple face. He was a little loopy from the Percocet.

"Let's go home and scare the neighborhood children," I told him as I took his arm.

It was strange to see my husband so vulnerable. I flashed forward to our old age.

Was this how it was going to be? I was only three years younger than Jim, so who knew if I would be the first one to become infirm. But I hoped I would be the one to take care of him, as lovingly as he had always taken care of his family.

When we got home, Eddie was ecstatic to see Jim. He didn't seem to notice anything wrong, and the dancing and their scratching ritual went on as usual.

"There he is. Hiya, monkey! I know, I know, I know."

Pant-pant-pant. Snort. Sneeze. Pant-pant-pant. Yelp.

But when Jim finally sat down on the sofa in the den, Eddie stood still by his side, looking at him with the intensity of someone who was trying to figure out if he'd met this person before. He eased up only when Jim talked again in his unmistakable deep voice.

Karin, Eddie's walker, was more rattled. She took one look at Jim and seemed queasy. For days afterward, she'd say her hellos and good-byes looking at the floor.

Jim stayed home the week, shuffling around the house with no particular destination, a heating pad hanging from his injured right shoulder like an appendage. He dozed off whenever the urge struck— in his reading chair in the living room, on the sofa in the den, at the dining table. Eddie stayed close. He and I found common cause taking care of our sweetheart. Eddie knew something was up and, whatever it was, he had to be in the middle of it.

Jim, meanwhile, was the perfect nightmare patient. His range of motion was so limited he couldn't even towel off by himself, but he insisted on taking showers and going up and down the stairs alone so that he could finally succeed in breaking his neck. He got cabin fever and wanted to go to work. He couldn't possibly go to the office, so he had to walk Eddie in five-degree weather with ten inches of snow on the ground. I accompanied them the first time out so I could hold the dog but Eddie soon started pulling on the leash to get back to the house. The dog was no fool. He wanted nothing to do with freezing weather. Jim tried to follow along but he walked at the pace of Frankenstein.

By the time we got home, Eddie was walking on three legs, dramatically holding one paw aloft.

"Everybody inside!" I said.

Good boy, Eddie.

Back inside, Jim made appointments with his doctors in the city for a few days hence, way too early to even think about taking trains. He asked for a beer while still on Percocet. He pet Eddie and then scratched his face without washing his hands. I applied ointment to his face wounds and Eddie licked it off. Soon I had had it with them both.

"Don't do that," I yelled. "You are risking an infection. And please go wash your hands. What's the point of putting antibiotic ointment on your face twice a day? Really, Jim."

Jim couldn't wait to get back on his bike. He first had to take it to the shop for a checkup and—oh, yes—heal.

"Of course I'll ride again."

I struggled not to slap him.

"I love riding and it's a great form of exercise. I don't want to give it up. Training- and fitness-wise, it's the best thing I've found."

It was hard to hear this when his stitches hadn't even come out yet.

"Right," I said. "Let's just wait for major catastrophic injury."

Sorry, hated to be a drag, but this was not fair to me either.

"I was pretty cautious, darling. I never went out without a helmet. I didn't go out when there was ice on the road. I've gone out of my way to ride on wider and safer roads. I want to have relaxing, fun exercise and I don't want to have to worry about my safety."

But, still, he fell. He still got hurt and came out looking so awful his own dog did a double take. Worse, we still didn't know the cause of the accident. Many days were spent trying to figure out what happened. Jim didn't remember much between the moments before the fall and the emergency room. That was the second fall of the ride, I later learned.

At a stoplight, he had tried to uncleat his right leg but lost his balance and fell like a turtle, on his back, with the bike still on the cleats on top of him. But he rolled over and did not hit his head. Jim remembered that minor spill, but not what caused him to squeeze the brakes abruptly a few minutes later.

Clemson saw no pothole, no pebble, no obstruction, no squirrel. Jim didn't scream. Clemson said he saw Jim's face as he was going down and it was blank, completely devoid of expression, as if he were already passed out.

Did he faint before the fall?

"What the fuck could have happened?" Jim asked Clemson.

"I looked at your bike and I can't find a major sign of mechanical failure," Clemson said, "which is why I'm wondering whether you had some kind of episode."

"Maybe something happened to the brake and when I touched it, it like seized?"

But the bike shop gave his bike a clean bill of health. A few days later we went back to the scene of the accident—a pristine bike lane along suburban mansions—and found no clues. Nothing.

"We may never find out," Jim said, resigned. "The accident was unsettling, but it was just a fluke."

"What would you do differently?"

"Nothing."

How reassuring.

Many friends who heard about Jim's accident had their own bizarre bike story to tell. Three of them were colleagues at the *Times*. They were riding, and splat. No one could remember a thing. Ever.

Jim felt well enough to go back to work after a week, but he was still in pain and I was still terrified of the bike. He'd already started riding the three-quarters of a mile to the train station.

"How about spinning?" I suggested. "We can buy a machine and put it in the garage. Or do Zumba with me. I've lost weight with the DVDs."

Jim pretended to be Eddie—deaf, dumb, and determined. He would ride again, when all the snowstorms cleared. He'd go looking for another ass-whipping, as they said in Puerto Rico. *"Buscando fuete pa' l fondillo."*

I prayed for more lousy winter weather.

Both the neurologist and the cardiologist eventually said he was good to go. This was after Jim took electrocardiogram and stress tests and shaved his chest to wear three sensors attached to an electronic device for thirty days. A special BlackBerry received the signals from the heart monitor and the information went automatically to the doctor. He looked like a robot, with wires coming out of his shirt. He had to sleep on his back.

"I guess this is good-bye," the cardiologist told him after getting the readings.

His heart rhythms were normal.

. . .

But among the medical bills that rained on us in the months that followed, there was a charge for treatment of a fractured nose. No one ever told us his nose had been injured. And his shoulder, which suffered his most debilitating and painful injury, didn't seem to be healing. They X-rayed it at the hospital, but they didn't find a break. His shoulder kept hurting. I suggested getting a massage, but Jim was reluctant. He thought whatever was wrong had not healed well enough and might get more damaged. He finally agreed to see my massage therapist for computer-related aches and pains, Dane, the gentlest and nicest. I had not seen him in ages, since I started regular yoga classes. Jim made an appointment, but after his massage he didn't feel any better. He complained of soreness for a week. Next, Jim went to see Wanda, a chiropractor friend of ours. She immediately told Jim to get an MRI. Based on the pain he was having and what she felt, she thought it was possible he had a rotator cuff tear. She wouldn't work on his neck or the shoulder because of the uncertainty about what kind of injury he had.

Finally, the MRI showed a non-displaced fracture, meaning there was a crack in the bone but the bone itself was not displaced. In addition, he had a tear of the cartilage of the shoulder joint. No wonder. There was nothing to do except take it easy. No need for a cast, just time to heal. But at least now we knew what was going on. Two months after the accident, we finally got the tally of the damage from the accident. But we never found out what happened. I was still relieved. Jim was still lucky. I was lucky. First Eddie, and now Jim. Even from my high horse I realized I needed to be a better person to my husband and to his dog because I was grateful to have them both in my life. Eddie was an extension of the husband. So were the children. I surrendered.

Jim soon got back on the bike in earnest and I joined him sometimes for short nice rides to nearby parks. We often dined alfresco like we did in L.A., in the beautifully landscaped backyards of friends. We had still not gotten around to investing in our own backyard to make it ready for prime time, but we hosted dinner parties indoors and were pleasantly surprised that we could get a quorum of friends from the city to hop on New Jersey Transit to make the trek to Montclair and back.

The next Father's Day, in spite of myself, almost without thinking, I got Jim a card, not from me, but from his dog.

"Dear Daddy," Eddie wrote. "Thanks for cleaning up my poop and laying out newspapers so I can pee in the living room. So convenient! I adore you and only you. Love, Eddie. Woof!"

That was written by She Who Routinely Purges Her Facebook News Feed of Friends Who Clutter It with Dog Pictures. But Eddie no longer brought out the worst in me. I bought wee-wee pads for the living room. I purposely dropped crumbs and cuttings on the floor while cooking.

My growing appreciation for our mutt meant that I worried more about him. When I exercised to my Zumba tapes in the den, Eddie still got all upset about the dancing. He tried to get me to stop by nibbling at my kicking feet or standing next to me—through the merengue, the salsa, the samba, and the reggaeton—and I was afraid of accidentally knocking him out. I put him outside and closed the door and after a few skirmishes he resigned himself to sleep through the workout.

Like old people, Eddie had some good days and some bad days. The visits to the vet became more frequent. Despite our vigilance, he once again ate something that caused another bout of poisoning-like symptoms. Another day, Jim went to take him for a walk and Eddie fell on the kitchen floor—just slid and flopped over and refused to go farther than the driveway. Even sick at the vet's office, Eddie managed to draw compliments.

"Pretty," said a woman who was holding a Labrador puppy waiting to get his shots. "I like his markings."

Some days Eddie seemed very low on energy and somewhat weak. Other days he was lively, rushing to his water dish after a morning walk as if he had just crossed the Sahara and was now ready to wolf down his breakfast. He had arthritis, an enlarged heart, and twenty other little ailments—and we had to clap to get his attention—but Eddie still got it. Only now it was a joy for me to watch.

Time served Eddie and me well. I didn't have that benefit with my stepdaughter and stepson, both already young adults in their twenties, and our relationships still needed work. There were thaws in their visits, but it was a struggle not to revert to old roles. That went for Eddie too. But as the humans around him came and went, he remained whatever we wanted to project on him. More often than not, he succeeded in revealing our best side to each other. Our solicitousness in walking and feeding him. Our concern for his health. Our capacity to laugh together at his antics and our sense of humor in trying to interpret his sounds, like when he was ordered out from underneath the dining table and into his corner and settled down with a "Harrumph!"

In our stepfamily, he was the champ. He was deserving of the term "family" after all. As Eddie hobbled around the house, restless even at his advanced age, sometimes I called to him and he responded like a normal dog, approaching semi-eager for my caresses. One day Jim found me sitting on the kitchen floor petting his dog and he smiled at the welcomed scene, as occasional as Halley's Comet. He had a look of melancholy.

"What?"

"Nothing."

"What?"

He hesitated, as if not to spoil the moment, then finally said: "He's forgotten he doesn't like you."

Epilogue

My husband and I have drawn closer from adversity. We just celebrated our ninth wedding anniversary. The marriage is steady, the family still a work in progress—isn't that always the case? Jim and I truly love each other, strengthened now by more than a decade of shared history. We know what we have, and what we don't want to lose.

The dog? Not so much.

Eddie is ancient—thirteen years old, a dog nonagenarian. As I write, he's resting a few feet from me, contorted into a coil on his bed in the den, licking his privates. He lives noisily on. He's pretty much the same self-absorbed "galoot," oblivious to my own personal transformation. He doesn't know he almost died, that I felt guilty, that his adored master also had his own uncomfortably close encounter with disaster, that I gained clarity about all of our relationships. He's our dog, for better, for worse, in sickness and in health, until death do us part. And who would have thought I would ever be saying that? Still, our relationship has yet to be upgraded to love-love.

I routinely pet him now, since we're cool. I'm still his meal ticket. I continue to feed him and I'm sometimes overcome, I admit, with motherly tenderness while he eats. He sounds like an avant-garde punk band—swirling the dry food around, smacking his tongue, pushing the bowl against the wall, hitting the bowl with his metal name tag—but the noise is comforting. Eat, doggie, eat, so you remain strong and ornery.

He still often ambles past me with nary a glance, stopping only to flaunt his perfect downward-facing dog.

Do I care?

No. He's senile.

Do I care that he snores more frequently and more loudly?

Only if he drowns out conversation or my favorite TV show. Do I care that he now sometimes lifts his leg toward me, rather than a stationary object like a wall, looking like Jane Fonda on all fours doing lateral thigh-raises?

No. He still can't reach me.

Do I care that he can't stay away from the kitchen and our legs, nose to the floor, "Checking it out, checking it out. Oh, that's interesting. Slurp."

Yes. I'm scared of tripping over him and killing him in the process, since he's increasingly fragile.

When I've had it, I lure him to the den, close the door, and don't let him out until we're through cooking. Jim sometimes sneaks over and lets him out sooner. Eddie's Che.

Do I care that when I let him out in the backyard he licks the grease from the grill, digs in our flower bed, and, lately, has started eating the wood chips that cover the dirt?

"Jim!"

I'm in the kitchen yelling at the ceiling. Jim comes down from our bedroom and I tell him about my discovery.

"Do you know what he's doing? Eating those wooden chips in the backyard! I had to pry one out of his mouth when I saw him chewing. That's what poisoned him!"

"Oh my gosh," Jim says.

Then to his dog: "What are you doing back there? Are you eating wood chips?"

Eddie keeps mum, but I'm certain I've cracked the case. That is, until I tell Jim's sister-in-law, Kathy, and she mentions that a dog of hers was poisoned once from digging up and eating daffodil bulbs. "Do we have daffodils?" I ask Jim. Yes, he says, and tulips and other flower bulbs that apparently have toxins and are poisonous to dogs and cats. Go figure. They must taste good. I go to a pet website to look up the symptoms of plant poisoning and there they are: vomiting, diarrhea, increased heart rate, abdominal pain.

Eddie is now forbidden from the backyard unless he's chaperoned.

I'm still at the *Times*, covering housing and still loving my work. Jim still works for *The Wall Street Journal*. Henry is still attending college in Southern California, and working part-time. Arielle is still working for an AIDS organization in Africa, still hooked on the continent. I'm sure counseling and therapy help many marriages. But in our case, so far we've made it out of the rough patches pretty much on our own.

Sooner or later, everybody grows up, even Eddie. My friend Tammy just visited and let Eddie sleep with her in the guest room, on his own cushion at the foot of the bed. Normally, that would have been an invitation for a midnight sneak attack. In a breakthrough, this time Eddie did not try to jump on the bed during the night, not even once, even though he's still capable.

Jim and I experienced a first—our dog made us proud.

Jim still rides his bike. He's now joined a group organized by his bike shop. They go out for rides of up to fifty miles in New Jersey, up and down hills, in and out of traffic, but at least he doesn't ride alone. I'm considering taking up biking myself so I can join them, even though I'm terrified of the cleats that lock feet to pedals. Jim says they help you propel the bike more forcefully, because you're not only pushing the pedal down but also pulling it up, making you more efficient.

"You use less energy per mile," he promises.

But learning to master cleats will undoubtedly require a few spills, and I cherish my bones.

I'm thinking about it.

After all these years, Jim is still the man of my dreams and Eddie is still the dog of my nightmares. We still catch him in flagrante on the sofa every now and then when we forget to close all the doors. He can't negotiate stairs, he's way past his expiration date—but he can still get his butt up on the sofa. He still fakes contriteness when we catch him there.

The seasons change, but my husband still wears rose-tinted glasses and Eddie is still Eddie. He still looks disappointed when I'm the first one down in the morning, and whimpers for Jim until he makes his appearance. Then it's ecstasy.

Eddie still flings himself against the stairwell door, repeatedly, trying to open it while we sleep upstairs. He's driven by the same old burning desire: to get into our bedroom, snuggle up to his sleeping beau and, at some point during the night, shove me off the bed. Jim still makes up great explanations for his dog's behavior.

"It's the change in weather. You know how when it goes from dry to rain, I get headachy."

I know.

Eddie and I still mark our territory and he still has the energy to bark at me occasionally. But his barking has less brio and I pretend it's good-natured and playful. I'm giving him a pass, for life. He's in his own personal la-la land. I enjoy the good and take the bad in stride. Whenever I see him standing still, stopped in his tracks in the middle of the hallway, as if he's trying to remember where he left his keys, I love him a little more. We're not best buds, but there's new mutual respect. We know we're not going anywhere. We've made our peace.

I still seek the soothing calm of yoga. One of my teachers talks one day about becoming an observer of our thoughts, as if they had nothing to do with us.

"Don't push them away," she advises. "The thoughts are going to come anyway. Step back and observe them and try to calm your mind that way."

I try it, but kicking my negative thoughts to the moon works better for me.

Kerri, my favorite yoga teacher, left for an ashram in India for five weeks and gave us a bunch of words to live by each week—inspiration, kindness, confidence, forgiveness—and a "power animal." The idea of the power animal is that of an ally, a spirit guide in animal form. They supposedly come to you in dreams, meditation, and in real life. Kerri gave us envelopes to choose from and I got the "dolphin." I was supposed to read up on it and see how I felt about it. I liked what I read. Dolphins remind us to breathe. They breathe in deeply, hold their breath underwater, and then breathe out with gusto. When humans follow their example, they release pain, anger, and other suppressed feelings. For the heck of it, I looked up "power animal" and "dog." Perhaps Eddie was in my life to fulfill a mystical purpose?

Nope.

Domesticated animals are too removed from their wildness and the natural world to be power animals, or so some of the spiritual animal experts say.

This is what Eddie would say about that: "Power animals don't sleep on sofas? That's not power."

I now appreciate dogs for what they really are: social bees. They can't be alone for a moment if you're in the house. They just want to be close to you. They make you the center of their universe. They don't talk, the perfect companions that way. No wonder so many humans go gaga for them.

When my dog-loving sister came to visit recently from Puerto Rico, I was eager for her opinion of Eddie. After hearing me complain for years, here he is, finally, in the flesh.

I let a full day go by before I ask her after dinner: "What do you think?"

"No, he's not too friendly," Mari says, looking at Eddie resting at Jim's feet. "He only has eyes for Jim. Now I know what you mean."

Thank you, *querida*.

"Would you ever get another dog?" she asks Jim as he rubs his mutt's head.

Jim closes his eyes and shakes his head. "No. Too much work. Too expensive."

Oh, but I know better, dear reader. I don't know everything, but I know my husband will always want a dog. Jim can't even help striking up a conversation with a random dog tied to a parking meter as he walks by. "Hi, buddy. Looking good."

I'll leave you with what else I know. Let's call it my Top Ten Do's and Don'ts when you find a dog in your romance.

10. Show you're not a competitor for food or affection—the dog, and the children, for that matter, should know right off the bat there will always be plenty of both for them, especially biscuits.

9. Throw yourself into the mosh pit. There's no way to avoid your instant family, even the four-legged members, so you might as well get in there and fight for your place early.

8. Carve out childless, dogless space in the house and the relationship.

7. Give it time. Stepfamilies don't mesh easily. It sometimes takes dog years.

6. Don't take anything personally.

5. Have sex.

4. Take a class, read a book, do whatever it takes to understand what's going on in the dog's head. It's not totally empty.

3. Do downward-facing dog. Yoga helps.

2. At your craziest, don't lose sight of yourself and your values.

1. And never, ever, underestimate the dog.

Recipes

Jim's Porcini Pasta

—•—

One package of dried porcini mushrooms.

Soak in a bowl of warm water for at least one hour. Once the porcini are resuscitated, remove and put them in a bowl and take the liquid they were soaking in—which should be dark brown and have a nice scent of porcini—and boil down by at least half to two-thirds in a small pot, and save for later.

Sauté some diced onion (one large onion or less) in olive oil until clear. Sauté in some chopped garlic, a few cloves, about 7 minutes or so in all. Do not overcook.

When ready, open up two 14.5-ounce cans of diced tomatoes. Pour off the liquid and then put the diced tomatoes in with the onions and garlic.

Stir and let the tomatoes mix well with the onions and garlic and cook down. About 7–8 minutes.

Once the ingredients are well cooked, put in the porcini mushrooms and some of the reduced porcini broth and stir well.

Let cook in an uncovered pot for about 7–8 minutes over medium-high heat, bringing the ingredients to a boil. Then lower the heat so the sauce is just slightly bubbling. Stir often to avoid anything burning or sticking to the pot. Cook for another 15–20 minutes or so.

Turn it off and let it sit on the stove for 15–30 minutes.

Serve over penne pasta.

Dinorah's Pernil

——

7 pounds pork shoulder, with fat (picnic cut).

Adobo—use mortar and pestle to mash 10 garlic cloves with oregano, pepper, half a cup of olive oil, one spoonful of vinegar, one envelope of Sazón seasoning, and salt to taste.

Make deep incisions in the meat with a knife and rub the adobo mixture into them and on the surface of the meat itself.

Marinate overnight.

Roast in a deep pan with the fat side up at 350°F for about 4 hours, uncovered, until brown and skin is crispy. (You can remove the crackling and put it back in the broiler for a few more minutes until extra crispy.) Break into serving pieces.

Titi Edda's Arroz con Gandules

Sofrito (a few square pieces of smoked ham, half an onion,
* three cloves of garlic, half a green pepper, and cilantro*
* to taste)*
4 spoonfuls vegetable oil
½ can tomato sauce
1 envelope Sazón seasoning
2 spoonfuls Goya "alcaparrado" (manzanilla olives,
* pimentos, and capers)*
1 can Goya gandules (pigeon peas)
2 cups white rice (long or short grain)

Sauté sofrito in vegetable oil. Add tomato sauce, Sazón, and alcaparrado. Add *gandules* and rice. Add water to barely cover the rice and *gandules*, stir, and simmer over low heat, covered.

Stir occasionally after water is absorbed until done.

Mia's Tostones

—•—

Peel 2 green plantains and cut into inch-wide pieces.

Fry pieces in vegetable oil until soft enough for a fork to go through them.

Take pieces out, dry with paper towel, and flatten each one into a round chip by pressing down with a plate or hand over a brown paper bag (since they're hot).

Dip each chip in salty water and throw back in the pan to fry again until crispy golden.

Serve with dipping sauce of ketchup with garlic, hot sauce, and cilantro.

Levona's Plum Cake

—•—

Cream one cup of sugar and a half cup of sweet butter by beating the butter and then slowly adding the sugar until the mixture is light in color.

Add one cup flour, one teaspoon baking powder, a pinch of salt, and two eggs and beat well.

Spoon the batter into a 9-inch springform pan.

Cover the top with 12 purple plums (pitted and halved).

Sprinkle lightly with sugar, lemon juice, and one or more teaspoons cinnamon.

Bake at 350°F for about an hour.

Cool and serve.

Acknowledgments

Stepdog started out as a personal joke, a way to deal with the stress of contending with a jealous dog, but people I respect convinced me that the voice in my head should be heard more broadly. My friend and colleague at the *Times*, Dana Canedy, was an early and constant cheerleader. She also introduced me to her agent, the incomparable Flip Brophy of Sterling Lord Literistic, who believed in the book and did not rest until she found the right publisher. That would be G. P. Putnam's Sons, where my editor, Kerri Kolen, and her team offered unbridled enthusiasm, thoughtful advice, and meaningful editing.

Also helping me keep the manuscript on the right path were my sister Mari Navarro, my girlfriends Tammerlin Drummond and Laura Rodriguez, and my friends and colleagues Jan Benzel and Bruce Weber. Another friend and colleague, photographer Monica Almeida, took the cover picture that captured a dog's spirit. And my childhood friend, Clemson Smith Muñiz, never tired of trying to get a dog's best side.

Thank you all, dog and cat people alike.

Most of all I thank my husband, Jim Sterngold, for being my true love and partner in life, and a really good sport. He nurtured this book as the labor of love it always was.

Lastly, I thank our dog, Eddie. He was always honest about his feelings, that's for sure, and he stuck around long enough to bring out the dog lover in me.

Couldn't have done it without you, mutt.